HC

HENRY VII

Jocelyn Hunt and Carolyn Towle
Series editor: Christopher Culpin

942·051

CONTENTS

PART ONE

TELLING THE STORY

Henry VII: what were the main issues of his reign?

Henry VII is often overshadowed by the more flamboyant kings either side of him: before him came the 'wicked' Richard III who was supposed to have murdered his two nephews in order to seize the throne; after him comes Henry VIII, with his exciting private life. Shakespeare wrote plays about English history all the way from the 1390s to the 1530s and yet 'left him out', as if he were too boring to make a good story. Even his pictures, as you can see on the cover, show someone who looks more like a middle-aged clerk than a king.

Henry is, however, a remarkable character. With no real claim to the throne, he became king; with no experience or training as a ruler, he governed England for 24 years. His reign is seen by some historians as a turning point, the dividing line between medieval and modern British history. He secured his dynasty so thoroughly that, even though the Tudors as a ruling family died out after his grandchildren – Edward, Mary and Elizabeth – every ruler of Britain since has been directly descended from him. Britain has had civil wars, but one king has not been overthrown by another in a civil war since 1485, and that tells us something about the systems and methods that Henry put in place.

The purpose of this book is to give you an opportunity to study some of the key issues concerning Henry VII:

◢ **Was he a 'medieval' or a 'modern' king?**
◢ **Did his reign follow smoothly on from the Yorkists, or was it a whole 'new look'?**
◢ **How did he rule the country?**

◢ How soon did he become secure on the throne?

◢ How completely did he overcome the threat of the 'overmighty subjects'?

◢ Why was financial security so important to Henry, and how did he achieve it?

◢ What were his relationships with foreign countries? How did these fit in with his other policies?

◢ Is it possible to discover what he personally felt he was achieving and what motivated him?

This section is designed to give you an overview of the whole reign. Later chapters will provide discussion of some key topics. The timelines identify the key events in summary form; you may find it useful to 'make these your own' by converting them into flow chart or 'mind map' format; or you might organise them under headings such as *economic*, *foreign*, *judicial* and so on. Key terms with which you may not yet be familiar are defined like this:

KEY TERMS

Economic policy is what a king or government does concerning the wealth of the country and the revenue of the Crown: this includes financial, or money policies, taxation, trade and commerce, and attitudes to farming and to the production of other goods.

Foreign policy covers government actions and ideas concerned with the relationship of their country with other countries, whether it involves war, treaties or any other links.

Judicial policy concerns the law courts and the systems in place for dealing with people who break the laws of the country.

When you have finished reading the chapter, select the FIVE points you consider to be the most important, and justify your particular five to the rest of your group.

The England Henry won at Bosworth

1 In 1485, England was recognised throughout Europe as a prosperous country. The population was about 2.25 million – smaller, in fact, than it had been before the Black Death in 1348–49. The low population meant that in spite of inefficient farming methods, there were no food shortages. Many foreign visitors commented on how well the ordinary English people lived, emphasising particularly how much meat they ate. The only large town was London, with a population of about 50,000 to 60,000. The other great towns of England, such as York, Bristol and Norwich, had about 10,000 inhabitants.

2 Most people made their living by farming, but the manufacture of wool cloth was developing rapidly. This was leading to a growth of towns and a slow, but steady, population drift towards the south-east of the country. The profits to be made from wool were also encouraging *enclosure*, with arable land being used instead for sheep rearing. This caused anxiety for the government for two main reasons: first, because rural unemployment could easily lead to unrest and rebellion; secondly, because the *depopulation* of some regions, particularly on the coast, could have important side-effects in case of war.

KEY TERMS

Enclosure is when landowners fenced in either common grazing land, or the shared crop-growing fields of the village. Many then used the land to keep sheep.

Depopulation is when people move away from an area; enclosures meant that fewer farmworkers were needed and so the peasants had to move to find work elsewhere.

3 England expected to defend itself with the militia (local people who trained in fighting skills on a part-time basis, and then could be called upon to fight in case of attack). This meant that the people of the North of England were often engaged in repelling attacks from Scotland. They expected, as a consequence, to pay less tax when money was demanded for other wars. There was no standing army, mostly because no king could afford the cost. As a result, the monarchs were prepared to some extent to allow the nobles to keep

large households of fighting men, since these could be useful in time of war. As you will see later, Henry had to balance the law and order risks of these 'retainers' against the need to have them available to fight.

4 Travel around England was not easy: few roads and bridges had been built since Roman times, and the maintenance of the highways had not been a priority through the years of civil war. This meant that even a royal messenger might take a week to travel the 180 miles between London and Exeter. Henry's *progresses* around England are all the more remarkable when you consider the practical difficulties of getting about with a large retinue.

KEY TERM

Progress was the name given to a formal journey by the monarch around the country. It had various purposes: one was for the people to see their sovereign; another was for the King to make an inspection of his lands, and feel the mood of the people. In the middle ages it had also been a way of spreading the cost of feeding the whole royal household, by travelling from estate to estate, instead of food having to be brought into London.

5 Other forms of communication were also very limited. Printing was beginning to develop but, at the start of Henry's reign, reading and writing were still generally the business of the church rather than of ordinary people. Nevertheless, literacy in the towns was accelerating, encouraged by the establishment of English as the main language for printed books and other material. This meant that a growing number of people could learn to read without also having to grapple with Latin or French. Henry VII was to take advantage of this growing number of readers by producing 'propaganda' justifying his claim and emphasising his achievements. Accounts of how Henry VI (the last Lancastrian King) had been martyred were printed and circulated; Acts of Parliament and Proclamations were published in English so that they could be read by local administrators and understood by the public.

Who was Henry?

Henry Tudor, Earl of Richmond, was 28 when he took the English throne. He was born in Pembroke Castle, Wales, after the death of his father, Edmund. Henry's mother was just 14 when he was born. He was descended from both the French wife of Henry V (by her second marriage) and from Edward III, through the third marriage of John of Gaunt, Duke of Lancaster (as you can see from the family tree on page 23).

The death of Henry VI in 1471, and of his son, made Henry Tudor a more serious Lancastrian claimant, and he went into exile in Brittany to avoid the threat of the Yorkists. Foreign policies at the start of his reign were to be guided by a feeling of obligation towards Brittany, which had sheltered him.

The accession in 1483 of Richard III was not popular with many of the important families in England: Richard was not the next heir, but the young sons of Edward IV were sidestepped, on the grounds that they were illegitimate, put into the Tower and never seen again. This caused several nobles to favour the Lancastrian claim, and Henry, living quite comfortably in Brittany, began to gather a 'court' round him. After one failed attempt at an invasion in 1483, Henry landed at Milford Haven in Wales in August 1485, and advanced into England gathering recruits along the way. Even so, he was outnumbered by Richard's army, or would have been had two noble families given Richard the support they had promised. In the event, the Earl of Northumberland kept his troops out of the fighting, and Lord Stanley (married to Henry Tudor's mother as her third husband) changed sides in the middle of the battle. Henry had little or no experience of fighting, but made a sound job of defeating the Yorkists. Whether Richard's crown was actually found under a thorn bush and handed to Henry, as Shakespeare suggested, is impossible to prove. Symbolically, however, the battle gave him the throne which no one, at the time of his birth, would have predicted would be his.

Henry's position as king

Henry's claim to the throne was dubious to say the least. You will have an opportunity in Chapter 1 of Part 2 to learn about his family and to study a simplified family tree, to see who else had better claims than he did. He had won the crown by force of arms at the Battle of Bosworth (22 August 1485), and from then on worked to ensure that no one else should do the same to him. He entered London on 3 September, and his coronation in October was a sumptuous affair. It was suggested that Henry had learned from his time in France the propaganda value of display. He also kept close by him his personal bodyguard, later to be known as the Yeomen of the Guard.

Henry's reign was declared to have begun on 21 August, so that those who had fought for the Yorkist King could be accused of treason. His first parliament recognised him as king without being precise as to what his right was.

Henry had promised while in exile to marry Edward IV's daughter Elizabeth of York, but he did not do this immediately, since he did not want it to appear that his claim depended on his Yorkist wife. After all, she had four sisters, so it was important that no one should imagine that the way to the throne lay through marriage. They married on 18 January 1486, although Elizabeth was not crowned queen until 25 November 1487. It seems likely that they cohabited before the marriage, as the first of their seven children was born in September 1486. He was named Arthur, after the legendary hero King.

Henry also ensured that the four sisters were no threat: one became a nun, while the rest were married to loyal men. The young Earl of Warwick, the only serious remaining Yorkist claimant, was kept safely in the Tower of London until Henry found it necessary, or possibly found a reasonable excuse, to have him executed.

Henry spent much of 1486 making a progress. He suppressed a couple of rebellions and risings, and by 1487 his position was strong enough to shrug off the threat of Lambert Simnel's claim, about which you will read more in Chapter 2 of Part 2. Later threats to Henry's authority tended to be more in the nature of anti-tax riots than dynastic risings, although in the 1490s some of the Irish Lords, together with the King of Scotland, made use of a claimant called Perkin Warbeck. By then, however, Henry was strong enough to survive, and the succession of his son in 1509 without difficulties is proof that the dynasty was firmly established.

Henry and parliament

Earlier kings had summoned Great Councils of the nobility when they needed advice or support. Henry did so too, but made more use of parliament, which included representatives of the common people. The House of Commons consisted of 74 representatives from the shires and 109 from the boroughs, or towns. Each constituency returned two MPs. These were not 'ordinary' people, since they were not paid and had to be able to leave their homes and their normal occupations for the duration of a parliament; the shire MPs were meant to be knights, and the borough MPs, or burgesses, were intended to be prosperous citizens. In many towns, landed gentry had taken over burgess seats. In a very real sense, though not in the modern sense, these were the *'middle classes'* of England.

> ### KEY TERM
>
> **Middle class**: historians use this term in a variety of ways. In modern history it is seen as meaning the same as bourgeoisie (town dwellers making their money from commerce and the professions, rather than from the land). It is, however, reasonable to use it in a more literal sense – that is, the people who were neither at the 'top' nor at the 'bottom' of society. In Tudor times this might mean the lesser landowners, or gentry, as they are sometimes known, as well as the town dwellers and members of the professions. This class would have some education, and a sufficient income to spare time for matters other than the harsh business of staying alive. The church was one of the stepladders by which such people could rise to important rank, but Henry also gave them opportunities through local government and justice, and through parliament.

Henry's first parliament met on 7 November 1485, very soon after his coronation, and you will be able to read in more detail what sort of work it did in Chapter 3. During his whole reign, of 24 years, there were seven parliaments, lasting a total of 69 weeks. All the parliaments met at Westminster, whereas in earlier times parliaments had met wherever the king happened to be at the time of the writ being sent out. This is perhaps a sign that the King was confident of the loyalty of London, and aware of the benefits of staying close to the financial and economic heart of his kingdom.

There was no protest at the infrequent calling of parliament or when the King ordered a *prorogation* after a few weeks. Over the previous century, the people of England had come to associate the summoning of parliaments with trouble (or tax demands at least!). The late fifteenth century was not a period when people longed for innovation or saw the need for legislation.

There is no indication that parliament was *'packed'* by Henry VII. Later kings and queens went to considerable trouble to ensure an easily managed House of Commons, but at this period there was a tradition of loyal service to the king: after all, parliament met only when it was summoned; being Speaker was a difficult and time-consuming task and the MPs were happy to have a royal official organising their work and sorting out all the business. Later monarchs were to find this situation much altered. This is not to say that Henry always got what he wanted from parliament without a struggle: there were disputes in several of his parliaments, notably over money in the last one in 1504.

KEY TERMS

Prorogation is when the monarch tells the parliament to stop meeting for a certain amount of time, but does not close it down; this means that there is still a parliament, but the MPs do not have a chance to meet or discuss issues.

Packing Parliament is the term used when the ruler makes sure that MPs are elected who will do what he or she wants; this can be done by bribes, or by threats.

Foreign affairs

Henry meanwhile was establishing his status as a ruling king by getting involved in the affairs and conflicts of the rest of Europe (about which you will learn more in Chapter 5). In 1489 he signed an agreement with the Spanish monarchs to fight against France, and in 1492 he actually led his troops to Boulogne against the French, in person. He demonstrated his abilities as a leader (which had already been established, after all, by his victory at Bosworth), by persuading the French to sign a treaty after only nine days of fighting. They granted Henry an annual pension in return for peace, while enabling him to keep almost half the war tax he had persuaded parliament to vote him. Another strand of his foreign policy was the need to prevent the various Yorkist claimants to his throne getting help from abroad. His relationships with the rulers of Burgundy, and with the Habsburgs, were affected by the help which Margaret, Duchess of Burgundy, gave to the pretenders trying to claim Henry's crown. The marriages of his elder son and his elder daughter into the royal families of Spain and Scotland also played their parts in his ***diplomacy***.

> ### KEY TERM
>
> **Diplomacy**: ways of organising and keeping friendly relationships between countries by using ambassadors and other contacts to discuss matters without going straight to war. (This term is more fully explained in Chapter 5, page 97, but this brief definition will be enough for now.)

Henry was aware of the advantages of having agents in foreign countries – namely to send back information and to get to know the people. This is the period in which 'nation states' may be said to have begun to develop. It is also the period in which diplomacy began to be seen as a normal practice of monarchs. Henry's treaties almost always included clauses to enhance trading opportunities, since Henry was always aware of the advantages of wealth.

Finance

'The kings, my predecessors, weakening their treasure, have made themselves servants to their subjects', Henry is reported as saying. His entire reign was one of careful accounting and the accumulation of wealth, which is discussed in more detail in Chapter 4.

- Trade was one of the many sources he tapped: he is famous for having rented out the seven ships of his navy to merchants during a time of peace.

- He was keen to find new sources of trade and, though he 'missed' the opportunity to sponsor Columbus in 1492, he supported the voyages of John Cabot which were to give England an early interest in the northern parts of the continent of America.

- In controlling his barons, Henry preferred fines to executions, and he made substantial sums through this merciful policy; in addition, he did not hesitate to collect various feudal dues, as his distant predecessors had done.

- The tradition was that the king's day-to-day expenses should be met by his own income as a landholder, and during his reign he worked hard to repossess royal land which had been given away or lost during the political shifts of the Wars of the Roses.

◢ Other regular sources of income included the customs duties on wine and wool, which parliament voted him for the whole reign, as well as the taxes which parliament authorised in times of national crisis.

◢ In addition, Henry found a variety of ways to 'borrow' from the barons and from rich corporations such as the City of London.

◢ The Church was another institution which provided Henry with money. The king was entitled to a share of the first year's revenue on the appointment of any bishop, and Henry became adept at moving his bishops around in a kind of profitable 'musical chairs'. He was also entitled to the revenue of vacant dioceses, and on several occasions delayed appointing a new bishop and reaped the benefit.

By the end of the fifteenth century, Henry was collecting about £110,000 a year (at a time when a skilled archer might be paid 6d a day, or about £7–£8 a year). Above all, he was very 'careful': it is almost literally true that he kept his money under the bed. Access to the Jewel House, where the wealth was stored, was through the King's own chamber. He adopted the revised administrative and accounting methods of his Yorkist predecessors and he was solvent from 1492 on: that is, his income exceeded his expenditure every year from then. Thus he was able to leave his son a throne which was financially secure, although it did not take Henry VIII long to spend his inheritance.

Henry and the nobility

Henry realised, from the start of his reign, that he needed to bring the barons under control, in order to ensure that they never again played one claimant off against another for their own territorial and financial benefit. In fifteenth-century England it was the noble families who held the wealth and the power. They controlled large areas of land, over which they had virtually complete authority. Here is a brief summary of what made the barons so dangerous:

◢ Source

The trouble in England in 1485 was that too many people owned dangerous weapons or knew where they could lay hands on them. If a man had a grievance against his neighbour he took it for granted that the courts of law would give him no help unless he bribed or intimidated the sheriff, the judge and the jury. Men who had learnt to rob, burn and kill in France could not settle easily to useful work when the Hundred Years' War was ended, and thousands became members of private armies controlled by powerful landowners. Each 'retainer' was required to fight for his lord without question, and in return he wore his lord's badge and received wages, food, ale and clothing. All this was called his 'livery' or what was delivered to him. In addition the lord promised that if the retainer was brought to court because of crimes committed in his service, he would 'maintain' his man's interests by all the usual methods of bribes and violence.

*From R. G. Brandon **A Survey of British History** (Edward Arnold, 1951)*

This was the problem which Henry needed to solve, and he did so with a range of institutions and laws. He made use of the opportunity offered by the various failed rebellions of his reign to bring Ireland more firmly under control, and to reduce the influence of some of the great noble families. At the same time, he made or reissued laws which outlawed the private armies of retainers and established courts which could not be intimidated or bribed. Towards the end of his reign his approach became less moderate, although still not particularly violent.

◢ Source

From now (1501) until the end of his reign, his earlier, and more generous instincts deserted him. He became almost pathologically frightened and brutally suspicious both of his somewhat withdrawn nobility and of his higher officials ... in the first decade of the sixteenth century, the list of nobles under bonds or recognisances [defined and discussed in Chapter 3], either for their own good behaviour or that of others, reads almost like a roll call of the English peerage.

*From Professor J. R. Lander **Government and Community: England 1450–1509** (1980)*

Some historians suggest that enough people in England were war-weary to make it easy for the King to bring calm to the country. This is contradicted, however, by Henry's obsessive anxiety towards the end of his life, and the gusto with which some nobles joined in the rebellions of his reign. It is also true that there were risings of one kind or another against every Tudor monarch, and noble families were involved in every one. In addition, even in the reign of Elizabeth (1553–1603) nobles were still being brought to court on charges of maintaining retainers in the law courts. It is equally true that no rebellion seriously threatened the security of the dynasty, and that may be taken as a measure of Henry VII's success.

Henry always employed men whom he had 'made' himself and who therefore owed loyalty to him alone. This is one of the points which leads to a debate among historians about whether Henry's style of monarchy was 'new' or simply following on from the methods and patterns adopted by his Yorkist predecessors. This is a subject which you will be able to debate and consider when you have studied his methods and his reign.

The last years of the reign

Although Henry's throne was secure by 1497, with the defeat of Perkin Warbeck's attempt to claim the throne, he suffered personal disasters which may well be one reason for his increasing cruelty and harshness in the last decade of his reign. In 1500 his youngest son Edmund died, aged only two, and in 1502 a potentially much more serious death occurred of the Prince of Wales, Arthur. From the dynastic security of three sons, Henry now found himself in the dangerous position of having only one son. The Duke of York, Henry, was carefully protected from now on, never ruling Wales from Ludlow as his older brother had done, and actually sleeping close to the King's own bedchamber. In 1503, Elizabeth of York died shortly after giving birth to their seventh child, a girl who did not survive. Some historians have suggested that she risked another pregnancy when she was quite old in the hope of bearing a son to replace Arthur. These personal losses may help to explain Henry's increasingly hard line against those subjects who might take advantage of any weakness in the succession. What is harder to explain or accept is Henry's unkind treatment of Arthur's widow, Catherine, who found herself so short of money that she had to sell her jewellery in order to keep herself and her household.

By the time Henry died in April 1509, England was secure, respected in Europe and strong enough to survive the more dramatic events which were to be a feature of the next reign. If Henry's main aim had been to establish his dynasty, he had certainly succeeded.

Henry's motives

What motivated Henry? Indeed what makes any ruler behave as they do? Some of Henry's motivations are likely to be the same as those of the rulers of the twentieth century, but some are bound to be different, and it is important to avoid ***anachronisms*** (like wondering how the voters felt!) when considering why he acted as he did.

KEY TERM

Anachronism: something that is wrongly placed in time, like a Roman soldier in a film wearing a wrist watch. Historians need to be careful to avoid using modern values and beliefs when trying to evaluate things that happened in the past.

Before you read on, turn to page 21 and discuss Henry's motivation as suggested in the task.

Timelines of the life and reign of Henry VII

Henry's life

1457 Henry is born, son of Edmund Tudor, Earl of Richmond and Lady Margaret Beaufort (28 January)

1471 Yorkist victory means Henry has to flee into exile in Brittany, where the Duke protects him from Edward IV's demands that he be handed over. Henry is now the chief Lancastrian claimant, since both Henry VI and the Prince of Wales died in this year

1483 Dubious circumstances of Richard III's accession make some people favour Henry's claim to the throne. Henry tries a landing in England but it collapses through a mixture of inept preparations and bad weather. Henry makes a public declaration that he will marry Elizabeth of York when he becomes king

1483–5 Disaffected English and Welsh gather around Henry in Brittany. People like Bishop Morton, Edward Poynings and Edward Courtenay show their allegiance to him at this stage. Propaganda campaign with Richard and Henry accusing one another of illegitimacy, usurpation, etc.

1485 Henry leaves Harfleur (1 August), reaches Milford Haven (8 August), and makes his way into England, collecting new recruits, via Shrewsbury, Stafford, Lichfield and Tamworth with no serious opposition. Reaches Bosworth with 6,000 troops
Battle of Bosworth (22 August). Henry wins. Enters London (3 September). 10-year-old Earl of Warwick put in prison
Coronation (6 November). Important that this should be before the marriage, so that no one can suppose he was king courtesy of a Yorkist

1486 Marriage with 20-year-old Elizabeth of York (18 January). (They need a dispensation, which arrives after the wedding)

1487 Son Arthur born at Winchester (20 September)
Elizabeth is crowned as Queen (25 November)

1489 Daughter Margaret born
Arthur is made Prince of Wales (November) (and Knight of the Garter, 1491)

1491 Son Henry born (created Duke of York in 1494)

1492 Daughter Elizabeth born (she died before she was three)

1495 Daughter Mary born

1499 Son Edmund born but dies in 1500

1501 Marriage of Arthur and Catherine of Aragon (14 November)

1502 Arthur dies at Ludlow Castle (perhaps from sweating sickness) (2 April)

1503 Henry's last child, Catherine, is born but dies almost at once. Elizabeth of York dies in childbirth (2 February)
Marriage of daughter Margaret (aged 14) to James IV of Scotland (8 August), following various agreements and treaties dating back to 1497. Not a happy marriage: first baby born 1507 but dies. The future James V born in 1512

1509 Death of Henry VII (21 April).

Key dates of Henry's reign

1485 Battle of Bosworth. Henry gains the throne and Richard III dies in battle (22 August)
One Year Truce with Scotland (October). (January 1486, extended for 3 years, and in fact continued till Perkin Warbeck appeared)
Coronation (6 November)
1st Parliament meets (7 November)

1486 Marriage to Elizabeth of York (18 January)
Henry makes a progress through England, establishing his authority and dealing with two small potential rebellions (March–May)

1487 Lambert Simnel and his 'handler' Richard Symonds arrive in Dublin (January)
Battle of Stoke: Simnel defeated and captured (16 June)
2nd Parliament meets (November)

1488 Small expedition to help Brittany against French aggression

1489 3rd Parliament (January)
Treaty of Redon. Commitment to help the new 12-year-old Duchess of Brittany, Anne, to resist France (February)
Treaty of Dordrecht: renewing links with Burgundy after Margaret of Burgundy's attempts to help Lambert Simnel
Treaty of Medina del Campo: trade agreements with Spain plus promise of Spanish Marriage for Arthur. Each to help other in case of war with France, effectively a promise to help Ferdinand of Aragon regain Roussillon and Cerdagne from France (March)

Anti-tax riots in Yorkshire, led by Egremont; crushed by Henry VII in person (April–May)

Treaty of friendship with Portugal renewed, and other agreements give England trading rights with Denmark and at Bergen in Norway, as well as the right to fish in Icelandic waters

1490 Trade Treaty with the Medicis set up a staple for English textiles in Pisa, but this leads to a tariff war with Venice which lasts until France's invasion of Italy in 1494

Maximilian Habsburg signs a military agreement with England (Maximilian was hoping to marry Anne of Brittany) (September)

1491 4th Parliament (October)

1491–7 Perkin Warbeck causing problems: claiming to be Richard IV, the younger of the two 'Princes in the Tower', he gets help or encouragement from some Irish Lords, from Burgundy and from Scotland, before being captured and imprisoned (November 1491–September 1497)

1492 Truce with Scotland resigned at Coldstream (November)

Treaty of Etaples with France. England gives up claims to all land except Calais; France promises not to help Warbeck and agrees to pay an annuity of £5,000 – in fact this will be paid regularly until 1511! (November)

1494 Sir Edward Poynings becomes Lord Deputy of Ireland (September)

1495 Henry's 5th Parliament meets (October)

1496 *Intercursus Magnus* signed with Burgundy: trade treaty very favourable to England (February)

1496–8 Italian explorer John Cabot begins Henry's interest in transatlantic exploration

1497 6th Parliament meets (January)

Tax riots in Cornwall turn into a full-scale rebellion, with the support and leadership of Lord Audley. Rebels reach Blackheath, on the outskirts of London, where they are stopped and defeated (May–June)

Perkin Warbeck is defeated and imprisoned (September)

1498 Treaty of Etaples renewed with Louis XIII (July)

1499 Perkin Warbeck is executed after trying to escape (16 November). The Earl of Warwick is beheaded (29 November)

1501 Marriage of Arthur to Catherine of Aragon (November)

1502   Polydore Vergil, an Italian writer, arrives in England (he composes a History of England which is one of the main sources on Henry VII)

1502–3   Henry's heir and wife die and his daughter Margaret marries the King of Scots

1504   7th Parliament meets (January)

1506   New trade treaty with Burgundy: so one-sided and favourable to England that it was known as the *Intercursus Malus*, and was replaced in 1507 with a more workable agreement

1509   Henry dies (21 April) and was buried in Westminster Abbey in the extension he had had built, where his wife already lay.

HENRY VII, *1457–1509*

This picture, which is in the National Portrait Gallery in London, was painted in 1505 by Michael Sittow. Henry sent it to Maximilian Habsburg as part of the negotiations about a possible marriage between Henry and Margaret of Savoy. Some say it shows his character as one of caution and coldness, but that might be just the way his hands are drawn. Certainly, he is shown with the Tudor Rose.

ELIZABETH OF YORK, *1465–1503*

Elizabeth of York by an unknown artist, probably made around 1490. This painting, too, is in the National Portrait Gallery in London. Her rich clothes are there to show her authority, and the Latin describes her as the wife of Henry VII. She is holding the white rose of York in her hand.

MARGARET OF BEAUFORT, *1443–1509*

Margaret Beaufort, Henry's formidable mother. This gilt-bronze effigy was created for Margaret's tomb by Pietro Torrigiano, the same master craftsman who had worked on Henry VIII's tomb. Her strong religious convictions are shown by the fact that she is dressed in the clothing almost of a nun.

TASK

Discuss with the rest of your group what you think may have been Henry VII's motives, and what constraints there were on his behaviour. You need to notice where points which would be relevant in the twentieth century are not going to be appropriate to the late fifteenth century.

When you have a list of headings, keep them by you until you have completed your study of Henry VII and then see if you would alter any of them, or rank them differently, in the light of what you have learned. You might compare your list to the one on page 55.

PART TWO

CHAPTER ONE

WHO WAS HENRY TUDOR AND HOW DID HE SECURE THE ENGLISH CROWN?

Objectives

◢ To understand Henry's claim to the throne and to evaluate its strengths and weaknesses

◢ To examine the way in which he secured the crown at Bosworth Field

◢ To explore what is known of the personality of Henry VII and assess whether his character was suited to the responsibility of personal monarchy.

Before you carry on, try task 1 on page 35. The purpose of this exercise is to familiarise yourself with the Yorkist and Lancastrian branches of the family descended from Edward III. It is also designed to enable you to establish some provisional ideas about Henry Tudor's position and claim. It will be particularly useful to complete this task if you have not already studied the Wars of the Roses.

The family background of Henry Tudor

Henry's paternal grandparents were Owen Tudor and Katherine of Valois, daughter of the French King, Charles VI. Little is known of the details of this extraordinary marriage. The match was so unusual because Katherine had previously been married to Henry V and after his death in 1422 she was Dowager Queen of England, mother of the new King, Henry VI. The circumstances of a dowager queen of French royal blood caused the Royal Council great concern in the 1420s. Such was the consideration given to her position that the parliament of 1427–28 passed a bill governing the remarriage of dowager queens. The statute stated that the king's permission was required for a remarriage, reflecting fears that it could cause problems, particularly if a new husband might seek to play a part in English politics. In the context of this

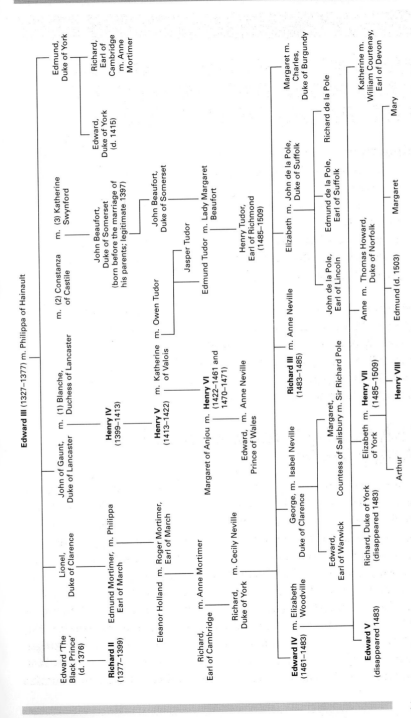

Figure 1 Descendants of Edward III: a family tree

statute, the subsequent marriage of Owen Tudor and Katherine appears even more remarkable, and it is not surprising that it was kept quiet. Owen Tudor was a man of modest Welsh origins who possibly met Katherine through employment in her household. Tudor family lands had been forfeited by statutes passed in the reign of Henry IV, but attempts were made by Katherine to promote her husband's pedigree and ancient lineage.

It is thought four children were born to the couple, with two sons, Edmund and Jasper, becoming significant figures at the Lancastrian court of Henry VI. The key fact is that they were the half-brothers of the King and were recognised as such by the Council. In 1452 Edmund was created Earl of Richmond and Jasper was created Earl of Pembroke, as well as both being endowed with profitable estates. They were the first Welshmen to become English peers. The Tudor name had risen quickly from obscurity through the involvement of Katherine of Valois. This meant that Richmond and Pembroke were closely related to the English royal family and had royal dignity but no English royal blood in their veins. So Henry Tudor had no claim to the throne through his paternal line.

It was the marriage of Henry Tudor's father, Edmund, Earl of Richmond, to Margaret Beaufort which provided their son with the claim of having English royal blood in his veins. You will have worked out from the family tree activity that Margaret Beaufort was the great-granddaughter of John of Gaunt, Duke of Lancaster, son of Edward III. The family name of Beaufort was created for the children of John of Gaunt and Katherine Swynford. However, the Beaufort line was of disputed legitimacy as Katherine was Gaunt's mistress when their children were born. An act of parliament had legitimised the Beauforts in 1397, but Henry IV had subsequently amended the statute, excluding the Beauforts from the line of succession to the English throne. Ultimately, it was well known to contemporaries that the Beaufort children of John of Gaunt were born illegitimate, and this potentially compromised their status. To conclude, Henry's claim to have English royal blood in his veins came, with all its flaws, from his mother Margaret Beaufort, who was married to Edmund Tudor around 1455.

◢ Source

The rise of the Beauforts was strikingly similar to that of the Tudors fifty years later. They were of royal blood but not fully so. They relied for their wealth and position on royal patronage, rather than on inherited estates.

From R. A. Griffiths and R. S. Thomas **The Making of the Tudor Dynasty** (1985)

Henry's situation before 1483

Henry was born on 28 January 1457 at Pembroke Castle, when his mother, Margaret, was just 14 years old. He was named after his uncle, Henry VI. Henry Tudor never knew his father, Edmund, who had died in November 1456, campaigning for the Lancastrians against the influence of Richard, Duke of York. Henry Tudor's childhood was dominated by the civil conflict known as the Wars of the Roses.

In March 1461 the Yorkist Edward IV claimed the throne, and Lancastrian forces all but collapsed. Owen Tudor was an early victim of Edward IV. Owen was part of the Lancastrian forces fighting to prevent the Yorkist ascendancy. Owen was captured and executed and the remaining Lancastrian loyalists like Jasper Tudor, Earl of Pembroke, were now fugitives, living mainly in exile. Lancastrian resistance in Wales was mopped up and the estates of Jasper Tudor were seized. Jasper escaped capture, but four-year-old Henry Tudor fell into Yorkist hands. He became a ward of William Herbert, Edward IV's chief lieutenant in South Wales. Effectively Henry was in custody, but he lived happily enough with the Herbert family at Raglan Castle, supervised by Herbert's wife. Herbert expected to marry Henry to one of his daughters. There is evidence that Henry received an appropriate education, although of course it was not training for kingship. Henry was still known as the Earl of Richmond, even though the estates of his father had been given to Edward IV's brother, George, Duke of Clarence. Henry was now separated from his mother, Margaret Beaufort. After the death of Edmund Tudor she married Henry Stafford, second son of the Duke of Buckingham.

Henry's relatively settled if somewhat reduced circumstances again changed in 1469. His fortunes became bound up in the struggles at court. Disaffection with Edward IV resulted in rebellion, led by the Earl of Warwick. In July 1469 Warwick defeated a royalist army, led by

William Herbert, who was subsequently executed. An unlikely alliance of the Yorkist Warwick with Lancastrians led to the restoration of Henry VI in 1470. During this brief period of Lancastrian rule Henry came under the supervision of his uncle, Jasper Tudor, again favoured by the ageing Henry VI.

However by 1471 Edward IV had reasserted his kingship. Both Henry VI and his heir, Edward, Prince of Wales, were killed. Henry Tudor was now the main Lancastrian claimant to the English throne. His safety could not be guaranteed by a Yorkist king. Jasper Tudor sought to protect his nephew and the two men fled to the continent, landing in Brittany in September.

Henry was to remain in exile for 14 years. He became hostage to the fortunes of the European powers of France, England and Brittany. (In Chapter 5 you will have the opportunity to study the complex relationships between these countries in more detail.) Most of Henry's time was spent at the court of the independent Duchy of Brittany, ruled by Francis II. Edward IV had two sons, Edward and Richard, and he worked hard to increase the security of his dynasty. He made various attempts to negotiate the return of the Tudors, who were a threat, particularly if exploited by a foreign opponent. At one point, in November 1476, Francis II nearly gave in to Edward's demands, but luckily the plans to surrender them fell through at the last minute. The Tudors remained in Brittany.

At this point what chance do you think Henry had of leading a successful rebellion and winning the English throne?

1483–85: winning the crown

The political situation in England again shifted dramatically following the premature death of Edward IV in April 1483. He was succeeded by his 12-year-old son, Edward V. However, by June the throne was seized by the new King's uncle, Richard, Duke of Gloucester, who became Richard III. He had challenged the legitimacy of Edward IV's sons. Controversy rages as to the immediate fate of the two boys, but there is no doubting the instability in English politics at this time. This meant that Henry Tudor, as an alternative monarch, became a focus for those discontented with Richard's **usurpation**.

KEY TERM

Usurpation is usually used to describe a situation where a throne is seized without authority or in opposition to the recognised line of succession.

Henry's position was more precarious than ever but, at the same time, potentially more encouraging. As early as the summer of 1483 Henry Tudor became central to a conspiracy against Richard III which involved key figures like Henry Stafford, Duke of Buckingham, and John Morton, Bishop of Ely. Buckingham had been a vital ally in helping Richard secure the throne but it was likely that he was now pre-empted by fears for his own safety.

By late August a 'Tudor movement' was emerging. Margaret Beaufort joined a conspiracy with Edward IV's widow, Queen Elizabeth Woodville, who probably believed that her sons, the royal princes, were murdered. The disappearance of the princes damaged Richard's reputation and was the key factor in transforming Henry's prospects. The destitute exile now had his claim taken seriously. It was at this point that the possibility of a marriage between Henry Tudor and Elizabeth of York was firmly proposed. Elizabeth Woodville promised to urge her Woodville friends and Edward IV's former servants to join the rebellion. Margaret Beaufort was in an ambiguous position. She aimed to promote her son's improved prospects, but her third husband was Lord Stanley, steward of Richard III's household. While Stanley travelled around the country with Richard III, Margaret stayed in London, organising the conspiracy. A messenger was sent to Brittany with cash and with instructions urging Henry to land in Wales as soon as possible, where substantial support could be expected. Henry was then able to secure additional financial support for an expedition from the French King, Francis II.

The risings of 1483 embraced groups in different areas of southern England, and ultimately collapsed in fiasco, partly through the difficulties of organising coordinated action. Buckingham's rebellion in the Welsh Marches also failed and he was executed without trial. Henry Tudor's fleet got as far as the south-west coast, before retreating: he must have been informed of the collapse of the rebels. After this Richard III worked energetically to improve his popularity and reinforce his position. He was now secure as long as he maintained the support of key members of the peerage: Lord Stanley, Henry Percy (Earl of Northumberland) and John Howard (Duke of Norfolk). Ultimately, greater responsibilities and rewards were placed in the hands of the few loyal northerners he could trust.

Henry Tudor was able to learn from the failure of the uprising. Thorough planning and named supporters would be required next time. Historians have debated whether the aborted rebellion enhanced or undermined Henry Tudor's position. He certainly gained from the death of Buckingham, who was a possible contender for the throne. Some argue that Henry's prospects were dimmed:

◢ Source

His value as a weapon in Francis II's diplomatic armoury had been seriously diminished; and, as Philippe de Commynes reported, Henry himself feared that Francis might now become reconciled with Richard III. His effectiveness had been shown to be the effectiveness of an impoverished exile whose allies in England had been soundly defeated.

From R. A. Griffiths and R. S. Thomas **The Making of the Tudor Dynasty** (1985)

Henry benefited considerably from the several hundred rebels who fled after the failed risings. John Morton went into exile in Flanders but nearly all the other rebels joined Henry in Brittany. Many were former courtiers of Edward IV. Their presence strengthened Henry Tudor's resolve to marry the daughter of Edward IV. On Christmas Day 1483 the exiles met at Rennes Cathedral. Here Henry solemnly promised to marry Elizabeth of York and in return they publicly dedicated themselves to the cause of Henry Tudor. Henry was further encouraged in the autumn of 1484 when John de Vere, the Earl of Oxford, escaped custody and joined the exiles. The Earl of Oxford was a popular, experienced Lancastrian and as such added weight to Henry's cause.

Richard III again focused on securing control of Henry Tudor from Francis II. Francis was old and vulnerable and in June 1484 Richard reached an agreement with Brittany. Fearing abandonment, as had so nearly happened in 1476, Henry fled to the court of the new French King, Charles VIII. By the spring of 1485 Henry had secured financial aid from the French government. He began to assemble and prepare an invasion fleet in the Seine estuary. In England, the future of Richard's dynasty had been undermined by the death of his son, Edward, in 1484 and the death of his wife, Anne Neville, in March 1485.

Learning from the 1483 episode, Henry tried to anticipate how much support an invasion force would have. Promises of help were rather meagre and hardly gave Henry much chance of success. However, it is likely that he had some encouragement from the Stanley family. Wales was again favoured as a location for landing, where Sir William Stanley, Lord Stanley's brother, held office and extensive lands. Despite the risks that these limited pledges suggested, Henry could not remain abroad: some exiles were growing restless.

On 1 August 1485 Henry's fleet left Harfleur and landed at Milford Haven in Wales six days later. It was crucial that the invading force, which included a French contingent, was soon strengthened. Messengers were dispatched to likely supporters. The invaders were in a precarious position: there was no automatic allegiance for a Tudor. The route had been carefully planned to avoid areas of southern and mid-Wales controlled by Richard III's agents. There was no alternative but to head northwards, via Aberystwyth, with the aim of entering England via Shrewsbury. Crucially, after about ten days marching Henry's position was fortified by the influential landowner, Rhys ap Thomas. It appears that Henry's promise of the Lieutenancy of Wales secured his backing. Henry's apprehensive force reached Shrewsbury largely unimpeded and advanced into England where a few more influential men joined him. But support from the Stanleys was still elusive. They sent money and at Stafford Henry briefly met up with Lord Stanley's brother. It is thought that Stanley made it clear he could not yet risk joining Henry Tudor. Richard III was holding George Stanley, the son of Lord Stanley, and if the family committed to the rebels too early, his life would be in danger. You can trace the route taken by Henry Tudor from Milford Haven to Bosworth Field on the map on page 41.

Henry was left with no choice but to move forward; his only possibility was quickly to engage Richard III in battle. Richard was at Nottingham Castle when he heard of the invasion. He had underestimated the extent to which Wales would stand aloof from the rebels. When he realised that Henry's troops had not been defeated, he moved to join his troops who were mustering at Leicester, probably on 20 August. Richard would also have wanted prompt action: each passing day saw the likelihood of further loyalties crumbling. Richard had been sending out orders to his subjects to recruit men, but his lack of trust is reflected in the fact that checks were made on the movements of unreliable gentry as they made their way towards Leicester. Richard was right to be suspicious because at Tamworth Henry was joined by two former members of Edward IV's household.

On 21 August the battle was imminent as the two sides closed in upon each other. Richard selected a site for the battle somewhere near Bosworth and pitched his camp early, resting his troops. At the same time more secret talks were held between Henry and the Stanleys, apparently discussing battle plans. Henry must still have had some anxieties and doubts about their commitment: only one man with Stanley affiliations had joined Henry. Before you read on, turn to page 35 and complete task 2.

1485 – the Battle of Bosworth Field

There are no eyewitness accounts and few useful near contemporary sources of the dramatic and decisive events of 22 August. Consequently, no historian has been able to produce a definitive description of the action. Polydore Vergil provides the most likely detail of who was present and the layout of the battlefield. Overall, the main reasons why Richard lost the throne were:

◢ lack of active support from the peerage;
◢ disloyalty at the battle of Bosworth;
◢ strategic mistakes on the battlefield.

Henry succeeded because of Richard's difficulties and errors.

It is hard to calculate the exact size of each army, but it is assumed that Richard did have an advantage in numbers. The royal army included a number of noblemen and powerful contingents of loyal northerners. Overall it was more formidable than Henry Tudor's mixed recruits and in a straight fight Richard should have easily defeated the challenger. But the situation was not as simple as that, as there were noticeable absences in Richard's ranks. After 30 years of civil conflict fewer than half of the English nobility and gentry were prepared to commit themselves on either side. The traditional sense of loyalty to the monarch had declined since the 1450s and less than half the peerage gave Richard III active support. John Gillingham (*The Wars of the Roses*, Weidenfeld and Nicholson, 1981) believes that 28 peers and many of the gentry ignored Richard's summons and stayed at home, awaiting the outcome of the battle. Few felt like taking risks for either man.

On the morning of the battle Richard's troops were positioned on slightly raised ground, known as Ambien Hill. The front-line of the royal army were commanded by the Duke of Norfolk. Behind these ranks was Richard III, with the bulk of the cavalry. The Earl of Northumberland and Lord Stanley were not given important positions, reflecting Richard's doubts about their loyalty. Command of Henry's troops was given to the Earl of Oxford. Fighting began early in the morning, with the rebels approaching the royal army directly. They came under strong fire from Norfolk's gunners and archers, and then the front ranks attacked, followed by hand-to-hand fighting. It seems the struggle was not convincing for either side. Norfolk's men withdrew slightly, leading to a lull in the fighting.

Henry and his bodyguard were then seen by Richard moving away from the main section of his troops. It is likely he was moving to make a direct appeal to the Stanleys. The implications were clear for Richard. Fearful of desertions, he decided to launch a direct charge on Henry. This action is regarded as a strategic mistake but other options were limited. His move was decisive at a time when others were standing by. A fierce battle around the two leaders ensued. Henry's standard-bearer was killed and Richard was thrown from his horse. At this point Sir William Stanley intervened against Richard, turning the course of the battle. His men were ordered to attack the royalist cavalry. Once Richard was dead there was little reason for his men to fight on: most fled or surrendered. The remarkable point about Bosworth Field is that loyalty and disloyalty were more significant than military planning or skill. The two greatest magnates in the country, Northumberland and Lord Stanley, who had benefited considerably during Richard's rule, did not join the fighting at all. Of those who were loyal to Richard, many were killed, including Norfolk.

King Henry VII: securing the throne 1485–86

Victory at Bosworth Field gave Henry VII the crown, but he still had to promote the legitimacy of his slender claim, win support and control the country. Ultimately, Henry was adept at putting his slim assets to his advantage and overcoming doubters. With few living relatives of his own, he relied heavily on friends and associates from his early life. He was scrupulous in rewarding those that had stood by him, but avoided extravagant gifts or titles: for example, Elizabeth Woodville had her privileges as a dowager queen restored to her. Parliament repealed the law which had previously confiscated her property, but Henry did not allow her to take possession of all the land; instead she was granted an annual income of £400 from the lands.

Trusted associates were depended on to establish Henry's authority in the provinces, become ministers and run his household. Part of Henry's success was the clever way he picked capable men of proven loyalty as officials of state. In March 1486 John Morton, Bishop of Ely, became Chancellor, emerging as Henry's closest adviser. The Earl of Oxford was placed in charge of the overall security of the country, with a prestigious range of titles: Chamberlain of England, Constable of the Tower and Admiral of England. Other key appointments included: Peter Courtenay, Bishop of Exeter, who became Keeper of the Privy Seal and Reginald Bray and Giles Daubeney, who joined the King's Council.

The Act of Settlement

Henry prevented any open discussion on the issue of the legitimacy of his claim to the throne, to suppress any continuing doubts. Henry's first parliament was compliant and a new Act of Settlement merely confirmed that the inheritance of the crown rested with Henry VII.

This first parliament met in November 1485, after Henry's coronation, so could not have been said to have granted Henry his sovereignty. Once the Act of Settlement was passed, parliament then repealed the Act 'Titulus Regius' which in 1484 had set out Richard III's claim to the throne. By removing this law the legality of Edward IV's marriage to Elizabeth Woodville was confirmed. By re-establishing the legitimacy and title of the children of this marriage, the way was open for Henry to marry Elizabeth of York. Henry then ordered the complete destruction of all copies of 'Titulus Regius', evidently keen to avoid stirring up sensitive debate about the relative merits of his and other claims.

Marriage to Elizabeth of York

Marriage to Elizabeth of York made good political sense. It brought about the symbolic reconciliation of the warring families of York and Lancaster. As with the first meeting of parliament, Henry ensured he was crowned before he married. Justification for his title could not be seen to have derived from a Yorkist who many regarded as the rightful Queen of England. Henry also learnt from the mistakes of his immediate predecessors, and the ill-feeling generated by the apparent advancement of the Woodville family; Elizabeth was largely excluded from government business. The marriage took place in January, following the granting of a papal dispensation to allow the union. In March 1486 a **Papal Bull** was issued acknowledging Henry's right and title to the throne.

KEY TERM

Papal Bull: a formal declaration by the Pope, with his seal (bulla) attached, usually dealing with some matter of faith or doctrine, though also used for political purposes.

Below is an extract from the Pope's communication. While you are reading it:

◢ note the reasons given by the Pope for confirming Henry's right to the throne;
◢ think about the reasons why the Pope would mention that the crown could pass to Henry's children of a subsequent marriage if Elizabeth of York died.

◢ Source

... his Holiness confirmeth, stabiliseth, and approveth the right and title of the Crown of England of the said our sovereign lord King Henry VII and the heirs of his body lawfully begotten to him ... as well by reason of his highest and undoubted title of successor as by the right of his most noble victory, and by election of the Lords spiritual and temporal and other nobles of this realm, and by the act, ordinance and authority of Parliament made by three estates of the land. Furthermore he approveth, confirmeth

Figure 2 Medallion of the marriage of Henry VII and Elizabeth of York

and declareth that if it pleased God that the said Elizabeth ... should decease without issue between him and her whom after that God shall join him to shall be had and born right inheritors to the same crown and realm of England.

Another significant action of Henry's first parliament was the re-enactment of the 1397 Act, which had declared the Beaufort family legitimate. (Look back in this Chapter at the section on the family background of Henry VII to remind yourself of the significance of this.) An act of 1407 which had prevented the Beauforts from claiming the throne was obviously quietly ignored. As the reign proceeded Henry became more overt in promoting his royal connections, because of the need to undermine pro-Yorkist propaganda. He made much of his mother's descent from John of Gaunt, son of Edward III. The Beaufort emblem, the portcullis, was widely used. Henry played on his Lancastrian background and linked himself with the growing devotion to the name and saintly reputation of the last Lancastrian King, Henry VI.

Henry dealt decisively with the defeated Yorkists although few were put to death. These included Viscount Lovell, Lord Dacre and Humphrey and Thomas Stafford who, as you will see in the next Chapter, were the first to challenge Henry's position.

TASKS

1 Use the family tree, on page 23, to work out the answers to the following:

◢ What was the relationship between:
Margaret Beaufort and John of Gaunt, Duke of Lancaster
Elizabeth Woodville and Elizabeth of York
Henry Tudor, Earl of Richmond and Katherine of Valois
Edward, Earl of Warwick and Edward IV
Edward, Earl of Warwick and Lionel, Duke of Clarence
Edward, Earl of Warwick and John, Earl of Lincoln
Elizabeth Woodville and Richard, Duke of York
Margaret of Burgundy and Richard, Duke of York?

◢ What claim had the following to the throne:
Richard, Duke of York (disappeared 1483)
Henry Tudor, Earl of Richmond
Edward, Earl of Warwick
John de la Pole, Earl of Lincoln
Edmund de la Pole, Earl of Suffolk?

◢ Using your answers provided by the evidence from the family tree, discuss in your group how strong Henry Tudor's claim appears, at the time of his challenge to Richard III in 1485. How strong were competing claims to the throne? You may alter your assessment once you have read further details in this chapter about Henry Tudor's background.

2 a How do you think the circumstances of Henry's early life and his experiences in exile shaped his personality and character?
  b To review the section 'Winning the crown', list those actions and events between April 1483 and 21 August 1485 which helped to advance the cause of Henry Tudor.
  c What were the weaknesses of Henry's position on the eve of the battle?

3 Personality and character of the new King, Henry VII
Below are selected extracts showing historians' views of Henry VII's personality, character and ability as a ruler. Read through the sources

and think about your answers to the following questions, which you can discuss with the rest of your group:

a What overall impression do these sources give of the character of Henry VII?

b In what ways do they agree or disagree about Henry's personality, characteristics and capabilities?

c On balance do his characteristics suggest that he had the ability to rule in an era of personal kingship?

d What would be the limitations of using only extracts of historians' writings? What approach could you now take to develop your own understanding of Henry VII's character and ability as a ruler?

◢ Source A

Henry VII was twenty-eight, tall, lean and fair, with thinning yellow hair, grey-blue eyes and bad teeth. He was, said the Venetian ambassador, 'a man of great ability'. He was ambitious, unscrupulous, devious, avaricious, astute, cautious and highly intelligent. Not violent by nature, he preferred to adopt a policy of reconciliation and pacification, but he could be ruthless when crossed.

A description of Henry at the start of his reign from
*Alison Weir **The Princes in the Tower** (Rodley Head, 1992)*

◢ Source B

… Henry cut an attractive and personable figure at the Breton Court. And in 1485 the Spanish merchants were able to take home with them an impression of a man who was still 'of pleasing countenance and physique'. They were the good looks of an alert and bright-eyed individual …

His experiences left their mark on him … he developed qualities of persistence and determination, astuteness and resourcefulness, which made him unabashed and unafraid when faced with adversity. He was capable of swift and decisive reactions, and yet he also learned the value of careful … planning.

*From R. A. Griffiths and R. S. Thomas **The Making of the Tudor Dynasty** (1985)*

◢ Source C

Henry's reign was distinguished by sober statesmanship. Bosworth's victor was a stabiliser: he could be ruthless and severe, but was neither bloodthirsty nor egotistical.

By comparison with Henry V, Edward IV and Henry VIII, he appears shadowy and remote.

*From John Guy **Tudor England** (1988)*

⊿ Source D

That [Henry] showed signs of promise as a future leader may be inferred from the fact that a number of [experienced] men did rally to him abroad after the debacle of the duke of Buckingham's rebellion. Schooled in adversity and disappointment as he had been, Henry had learnt to bide his time, to calculate his chances, to be cautious and suspicious, and yet to attract and bind to himself the support of diverse men whose aid might ... be invaluable.

*From S. B. Chrimes **Henry VII** (1972)*

⊿ Source E

The personality of Henry VII remains shadowy and elusive today, just as it was to his own subjects in 1485 ... He emerges from history books as a rather enigmatic character ...

*From C. Rogers **Henry VII** (1991)*

⊿ Source F

We are accustomed to think of Henry as a silent, grave man ... but this is only part of the picture. It is true that he cultivated discretion to such a point that men could never be certain what he was thinking, but he also had something of his granddaughter Elizabeth's liveliness of wit, and he was very fond of music ...

*From Roger Lockyer and Andrew Thrush **Henry VII** (1997)*

What ideas did you come up with as a group to further your understanding of Henry VII's ability and character? (Question **3d**) On the surface you might think that you have built up quite a strong impression of Henry VII as many of the points made by the historians corroborate each other. However, as Ian Dawson has clearly shown ('Henry VII – out of the shadows?', *History Review*, No. 22, September 1995), the student should be cautious in using such information in isolation. You will know from your GCSE studies that you should be prepared to think about from what sources the historian derived his or her ideas and views. The best contemporary description of Henry VII is that recorded by Polydore Vergil, who was quite balanced in his judgement (as we have commented elsewhere in this book). You will certainly want to look at this and other contemporary accounts as part of your further reading. Ian Dawson also emphasises the importance of placing Henry's character and abilities within the context of Henry's perceptions of the problems he faced, the actions he took and the policies he pursued at different stages of his reign. His personality and character were surely not static. As you go on to read about Henry's policies and actions, consider the evidence you are gathering to develop your own understanding of Henry VII. Only then will you get beyond the generalisations of the miserly, serious King.

CHAPTER TWO

SECURING THE DYNASTY: HOW SERIOUS WERE THE CHALLENGES TO HENRY'S RULE?

Objectives

◢ To examine in detail the attempts made to overthrow Henry, and to consider why they failed

◢ To study a narrative primary source and to assess its strengths and weaknesses as evidence.

Before you read about and study the events of 1487 and 1495–99, try task 1 on page 47. This will give you a clearer idea of the reasons why they failed and Henry VII survived. Use your list to evaluate the various rebellions confronting Henry, as you study them.

The background to the pretenders' rebellions

Henry VII faced two serious Yorkist rebellions in his reign. But there were other attempts to overthrow him which did not depend on the existence of an alternative claimant for his throne, so that for the first half of his reign he cannot have felt very secure. As we have seen in Chapter 1, Henry's claim to the throne was not a strong one; on the other hand, there were few other candidates available who might replace Henry. The young Earl of Warwick was safely in the Tower of London and Elizabeth of York was, apparently, happily married to the new King, with children being born to the match. The Courtenays and de la Poles seemed to be resigned to the Lancastrian-Tudor accession. The secure detention of any potential claimant remained a preoccupation of Henry's throughout his reign. In 1506, Henry negotiated the handing over of Edmund de la Pole, who was then kept in the Tower until Henry VIII had him executed in 1513. Similarly, from 1507 until the end of the reign, the Marquis of Dorset and Lord William Devonshire were moved from the Tower to Calais Castle to limit the numbers of significant prisoners kept in London.

There were always other threats to Henry's newly established control, however. Some were intent on keeping the uncertainty of the previous decades, which they had found helpful to their own ambitions: the Scottish King, for instance, and the Irish Lords who resented English attempts to rule them. Others were convinced that their opportunities for personal gain would be greater under a restored Yorkist monarchy, and it was a small group of these – Viscount Lovell and the Stafford brothers – who had first threatened Henry's new reign. A third group were those who were personally loyal to the Yorkist family: Margaret of Burgundy is the clearest example of these people, but those who joined in the various attempts to overthrow Henry VII are likely to have been motivated in part at least by a commitment to the memory of Edward IV.

Henry's progress through England

Henry's progress, begun in March 1486, was in part an attempt to change these loyalties, by showing himself to his people. It would also enable him to gauge the mood of the country, particularly in the eastern and northern counties, where he could not use his Welsh roots and influence as an instrument of control. The fact that he left his wife behind could be explained by the fact that she was pregnant, though it is also possible that he did not want her to be the focus of Yorkist affection. He travelled to Cambridge, where he was warmly welcomed, and then via Stamford, to Lincoln, where he spent Holy Week. In the Cathedral, he washed the feet of 29 poor people, one for each year of his life. (Discuss task 2, page 47.)

From Lincoln, Henry travelled to York, visiting Nottingham and Pontefract on the way. By the time he reached York, on 22 April, Lord Lovell had decided not to risk open rebellion, and had escaped. Lovell went to Burgundy where he found ready employment with Margaret, who seems to have been encouraged in her attempts to overthrow Henry by Lovell's presence.

Meanwhile, the Stafford brothers had risen in rebellion near Worcester, despite the fact that Henry was more confident of support in the west of the country. Henry advanced from York, and the Staffords fled into **sanctuary** as he approached.

The King took firm action, ordering the brothers to be removed from sanctuary, and executing the older brother. Protests to the Pope about the violation of sanctuary were not successful: Innocent VIII was aware

Figure 3 England and Wales in the reign of Henry VII

KEY TERM

Sanctuary means that the teachings of the Church allowed for someone wanted by the law of the land to ask for God's protection by taking shelter in a church or monastery.

of abuses of the system, and in August he issued a Papal Bull which severely limited the right to sanctuary, excluding it completely in cases of treason, thus vindicating the King's action. Henry travelled on meanwhile, via Hereford, Gloucester and Bristol and so back to London. He must have been pleased at the ease with which he had dealt with his opponents.

Lambert Simnel

More serious trouble was about to develop, however. John de la Pole, Earl of Lincoln (see the family tree on page 23), had been disappointed by the treatment he had received from the new King. By now, he thought, the young Earl of Warwick must be dead. This would there-fore provide an opportunity for someone to impersonate him.

The Book of the Houth (see task 4 on page 47) makes overcoming Simnel look quite easy, but Henry had clearly been worried. In January 1488, at his request, Innocent VIII ***excommunicated*** all the Irish priests who had been involved in the coronation of Simnel but Henry did not take any other action in Ireland at this stage: the Earl of Kildare remained as Lord Deputy until 1492.

KEY TERM

Excommunication is when a member of the Christian Church is excluded from all the rites of the Church and thus from the benefits of membership, including salvation after death.

In England there was a flurry of fines, but few executions. Henry need-ed little excuse to keep Yorkists such as the Marquis of Dorset and the young Earl of Warwick in prison. The Dowager Queen, Elizabeth Woodville, was placed in a convent, where she remained until she died in 1492. You may think that the later, more serious, attempt using Perkin Warbeck as a figurehead was undertaken because Henry had been so merciful earlier. On the other hand, Henry might have risked more serious resistance if he had embarked on a blood bath; and we may assume that he was always aware of the contrast between his mild approach and the supposedly bloodthirsty reign of Richard III.

For the next few years, what little resistance there was to Henry focused only on taxation. The levy which parliament agreed (January 1489) for his war against France was resisted in the north. The people of the north were expected to prevent invasion by the Scots, and so were not normally called upon to pay taxes for other wars. Lord Egremont used the opposition to the taxes to attempt a rebellion but Henry in person led the troops which crushed the rising.

Perkin Warbeck and foreign intervention

The most serious threat to Henry's position began in a quiet way in November 1491, when Perkin Warbeck arrived in Cork, in Southern Ireland. Originally from Tournai, in Flanders, Warbeck had been 'trained' for his role by Edward Brampton. Brampton came from an unusual background for someone about to dabble in English politics. He was a Jew of Portuguese origins, who had converted to Christianity in England. He now travelled to the Netherlands, where he collected Warbeck, who went with him to Portugal in 1487. Warbeck learned all about Edward V's brother, Richard, last seen in the Tower of London during the reign of their uncle, Richard III. The story was to be that Richard, Duke of York, had escaped from the Tower and ought now to be accepted as Richard IV by loyal Yorkists, since his brother Edward V was dead. One of the few advantages that Henry had in the crisis years was that Brampton returned to England and was able to tell Henry that Warbeck was definitely an imposter. The murder of the Princes in the Tower remains a mystery and has been blamed on all sorts of people. Josephine Tey suggests that Henry himself may have been responsible, in which case he would have been certain that Perkin Warbeck was not who he claimed to be. If, on the other hand, Henry did not know the actual fate of the Princes in the Tower, it would have been reassuring for him to be told by Brampton that Warbeck was not a true Yorkist prince.

Warbeck failed to get much support in Ireland, the Irish Lords presumably still feeling sensitive after the Simnel business, and in March 1492 Warbeck left Ireland and went to Paris. It was now (June 1492) that Henry replaced the Earl of Kildare as Lord Deputy. The new Deputy, the Archbishop of Dublin, Fitzimons, could be depended on to keep Ireland under control. In Paris, Warbeck was accepted as Richard, Duke of York. France was never short of reasons for taking an anti–English line, and at this point there was French displeasure at Henry's support for Brittany (which is discussed in Chapter 5; the reasons for his pro-Brittany stance were explained in Chapter 1). New developments in foreign affairs led to changes in policy and France soon lost interest in

Warbeck. At the end of 1492 he was ordered to leave France, going instead to the Netherlands, where his 'aunt' Margaret of Burgundy took over and intensified his training.

Warbeck's presence in the Netherlands led, among other things, to a trade dispute which damaged both England and Burgundy, which was only settled in 1496. Maximilian was torn: should he help Henry by disposing of Warbeck, in the hope that Henry would repay him in fighting against France? Or should he back Warbeck's claim and hope to gain control of a newly Yorkist England? Certainly Warbeck was making generous promises about the concessions which he would give to the Habsburgs once he was king. In November 1493, Maximilian recognised Warbeck as King of England.

Henry tried to limit the damage Warbeck could do by increasing royal control over Ireland (see Chapter 3) and by imprisoning or executing some of his more dangerous opponents – including Sir William Stanley.

In June 1495, Perkin Warbeck made his first attempt to take the throne. A landing at Deal in Kent, which was to be followed by a triumphal march to London, failed from the start, when he was prevented from landing. After a brief pause in Ireland, Warbeck arrived in Scotland (November) where he seemed to have struck gold. James IV welcomed him warmly, and treated him as a king. Warbeck even married the lovely Lady Catherine Gordon, cousin to James IV. James had a choice during 1496 as Henry proposed a marriage treaty with his daughter Margaret, but James preferred to back Warbeck. If Warbeck had synchronised his attack with the trouble that was brewing in the west of England, it is even possible that he might have succeeded; but by the time his Scots-financed troops were ready to move against England, the Cornish rising was over.

Rebellion in Cornwall

In May 1497, trouble flared at Bodmin. The Cornish, always reluctant to take orders from London, were deeply resentful of the parliamentary levies for a distant war against Scotland, about which they knew little and cared less. One of their leaders, Thomas Flamank, demanded – rhetorically – why they should be 'grounded to powder' over a 'little stir of the Scots soon blown over'. Led by Flamank, and another

Figure 4 Perkin Warbeck

Figure 5 Margaret Tudor, Henry VII's eldest daughter

middle-class man, Michael Joseph, they headed east, collecting Lord Audley as their noble figurehead on the way. Little blood was shed, though a tax collector was killed at Taunton. On 16 June, tenth anniversary of the Battle of Stoke, they camped at Blackheath, where the royal troops dealt with them. The rebels lost 1,000 dead, compared to the King's 300, and most of their leaders were captured or killed. Lord Audley was beheaded, though many other leaders and sympathisers were merely fined heavily, in what was becoming Henry's typical style.

Warbeck's failure

As a result of Henry's lenient approach, the area was at peace when, on 7 September, Perkin Warbeck landed in Cornwall. Ill feeling against Henry was strong enough for him to get as far as Exeter and then Taunton unimpeded, but there was no question of thousands flocking to join him and he was forced to surrender at Beaulieu. Six years of optimism and planning had come to nothing, and the half-hearted and uncoordinated help of Burgundy, France and Scotland had not been enough to topple Henry.

The end of Warbeck

Warbeck was required to make a public confession in the presence of Henry, who had it published and distributed around England and Europe, indicating, perhaps, that Henry had been alarmed by the incident. 'This unhappy imp', as the *Great Chronicle of London* calls him, was then put in prison. He was allowed some freedom at first, but after trying to get away was put in the Tower. In November 1499 he was found guilty of trying to escape with the Earl of Warwick, and was hung, drawn and quartered on the 16th. Warwick was beheaded two weeks later. It is not clear whether there were genuine plots to release the two, or whether Henry seized the opportunity to get rid of the last Yorkist with a strong claim. Certainly the government knew all about what they were planning. Some historians conclude from this that an agent was used to trick them into the escape attempt.

In 1502, Yorkists both in England and abroad were to claim that the death of Prince Arthur was a sign of God's displeasure and a divine revenge for the death of the Earl of Warwick. But Henry still had a male heir and his throne was in fact secure. You may think that neither of the pretenders, nor any other rising, actually posed a serious threat at all.

TASKS

1 Discuss and identify what would be the key ingredients for a successful rebellion. You might compare your list to the one on page 55 when your discussion is complete. Use your list to evaluate the various rebellions confronting Henry VII.

2 What ceremony do modern rulers of England observe, as the only remaining part of the traditional Maundy Thursday celebrations? What is the link between these rituals and the Christian Gospel story of Holy Week? For what reasons would English kings have performed these rites?

3 With a partner, study the map on page 41. Follow the route of Henry's progress, an extensive one, considering the difficulties of travel in fifteenth-century England. How important do you think the actual presence of the king was to the success of the progress? In what sense can we say the progress was a success?

4 **Studying a source**
Here are some extracts from an account written for an Irish lord sympathetic to Tudor rule. It was written in the early 1490s, and tells the whole story of Lambert Simnel. As you read the story:
   a Make sure you know what all the words mean as they are used here: usually you can deduce the meaning from the context. Some of the more obscure words have been highlighted in the text.
   b Work out who is meant by 'King Edward IV's sons' (line 6); Lady Margaret (line 17).
   c Decide what the writer thought were the motives of Richard Symonds.
   d Explain what, according to the writer, made Simnel suitable for the impersonation.
   e Decide what the writer's attitude was towards both Lambert Simnel and Henry VII, and find quotes to back up your conclusions.
   f Show how the writer displays his loyalty to his patron, Nicholas, Lord of Houth.
   g Sum up, in your own words, the reasons given here to explain how and why Henry VII was able to ensure that Lambert Simnel's attempt on the throne failed.

h Consider the reliability of the source. How does the writer's personal loyalty and his obvious bias affect the usefulness of the source?

◢ Source

There was a priest called Sir Richard Simon in the second year of Henry VII, that worthy Solomon. This priest had elected a scholar named Lambert Simnel, one of a gentle nature and **pregnant wit**, to be the organ of his **feigned** enterprise, and to be the rightful inheritor to the Crown of England and so thereof to make him King of England and to make himself to be some great bishop and **potestate** [sic]; for that, [he] craftily feigned King Edward IV's sons were away fled and thought to feign this scholar to be one. This crafty and subtle priest brought up his scholar with princely behaviour and manners, literature declaring to this child what lineage he was of and **progeny** [family], in so learning him he might so inform the people, that they should rather conceive the tale to be true.

Soon after, he caused to be blown abroad that Edward the young Earl of Warwick was broken out of the Tower, which both was of one years and one stature, and then he changed the child's name and called him Edward after the name of the young Earl of Warwick. And he with this child sailed into Ireland and there he declared this same to certain of the nobility there, which did both credit the matter and favoured the cause … And so they called him King … and so sent their letters secretly into England and also to Flanders, to Lady Margaret, sister to the King Edward, late wife of Charles, Duke of Burgoyne, to further his purpose with all his might and power. Sir Nicolas, Lord of Houth, perceiving all this but a mad dance, sent over to the King and **advertised** him of all these matters from the beginning to the ending who was the doers and maintainers of the whole matters in Ireland and Flanders.

After the King called his council and these thought good to give a general pardon to all those that would receive this same without any condition or exception. And after the young Earl of Warwick was brought to Paul's Church through London where as ever many might see him that thought he was run away and that they might perceive the **fondness** of those of Ireland to move war against the King without any just matter … The King, hearing these men's landing, concluded to encounter with them **incontinent**, lest that in long **tarrying** might enlarge their power and to increase being but a few in the beginning, which was a great cause of mistrust. To be short, both the armies came within a little to Stoke and the morrow after joined and fought very valiant on both sides, for those **allmayns** were very good and apt soldiers, so were their captain Martin Swarthe: his like was not in both the armies to all purposes. The Irishmen did as well as any naked men could do and at length they were slain, about four thousand

and more … *This feigned King and crafty Priest his master was taken alive. The priest was commanded to perpetual prison, and this innocent child became falconer to the king after. This field was fought the 16 of June 1487.*

After [in fact this happened in 1494] *the King sent for all his lords of Ireland, being in England with the King. After long talk with them the King said to the Lords, 'My masters of Ireland, you will crown apes at last …' This same day at dinner, where as those Lords of Ireland was at Court, a gentleman came where as they were at dinner, and told them that their new King Lambert Simnel brought them wine to drink and drank to them all. None would have taken the cup out of his hands, but bade the great devil of hell him take before that ever they saw him. 'Bring me the cup if the wine be good,' said the Lord of Houth, being a merry gentleman, 'and I shall drink it off for the wine's sake and mine own sake also; and for thee, as thou art, and so I leave thee, a poor innocent.'*

> From **The Book of the Houth** *(Irish history of the sixteenth century, produced by supporters of Nicholas, Lord of Houth). Quoted in Ian Arthurson **Documents of the Reign of Henry VII** (1984)*

5 Why was Warbeck's rebellion the last?
After 1499, Henry was not threatened by any other rebellion; while there were to be risings against specific policies in the reigns of Henry VIII and Edward VI, the next attempt to replace a Tudor monarch with someone else was to be in 1553 (Lady Jane Grey).

a Look once more at your own 'recipe for a successful rebellion' or at the list on page 55. Make a table with what was needed on one side; opposite each point, note down Henry's response, or the lucky circumstances which ensured that Warbeck failed.

b Write a summary showing the extent to which Henry had ensured that there would not again be any attempt to replace him. Also summarize the policies he followed which strengthened his own position while weakening, or making irrelevant, the forces potentially against him.

Answering examination questions based on sources

Examination questions based on sources come in a range of formats. They are all, however, looking for competence in various fields:

◢ Have you understood the various terms used in the sources?

TASKS

- Can you evaluate the reliability of the sources, using your knowledge of the period to discern any bias in contemporary sources; do you recognise and comment on any stereotyping or exaggeration in these sources?
- Are you able to make sound comparisons or contrasts between the varying points of view you are offered?
- How do you use your own knowledge, understanding and wider reading to shed light on the information and comments offered in the sources?
- What use do you make of the similarities and differences between sources which are primary and those which are secondary?
- Are you able to write an appropriate amount, and at an appropriate depth for the number of marks on offer? Some of these questions have more 'part questions' than others, so timing is crucial.

Here is a question used in 1986 by the University of Cambridge Local Examinations Syndicate. You will find that the language of the questions has changed only slightly over the years. You have about 40 minutes to answer this kind of question, allowing for 'read through time'. When you have attempted it, you may wish to read through the comments below, and discuss your answers with others in your group.

Document A

... not forgetting the great malice that the Lady Margaret of Burgundy beareth continuously against us, as she showed lately in sending hither of a feigned boy, surmising him to have been the son of the Duke of Clarence ... and foreseeing the perseverance of the same her malice by the untrue contriving of another feigned lad, called Perkin Warbeck, born at Tournai in Picardy, which at first went into Ireland and called himself the bastard son of King Richard; after that the son of the said Duke of Clarence; and now the second son of King Edward IVth ...

Letter from Henry VII to Sir Gilbert Taylor, 20 July 1493

Document B

Friday the 3rd of July, the so called Duke of York came to England with all the ships and troops he had been able to obtain from the Duchess Margaret, the Archduke and Flanders. A portion of his troops disembarked, but the people rose up in arms against them without the intervention of a single soldier of the King. The peasants of the adjacent villages made great havoc on the troops who had been disembarked, and if the vessels had not been at hand, not a single man of them would have escaped alive. A hundred and fifty were slain and eighty made prisoners ...

> *Letter from the Spanish envoy, de Puebla,*
> *to Ferdinand and Isabella, 19 July 1495*

◢ Document C

In the middle of these events (1497), Pedro de Ayala ... came to Scotland, sent by Ferdinand, King of Spain, to King James, to negotiate a peace between the kings of England and Scotland. For Ferdinand and his wife Isabella ... had the most friendly feelings towards King Henry, wishing him well, and anxious to make a marriage alliance with him ... After long discussions it was found impossible to agree upon any peace terms. This was because King Henry insisted that Peter Warbeck should be handed over to him. On the other hand, King James specially urged that he could not hand Peter over into the hands of his enemy: although James was at last beginning to be aware of Margaret's deceit, but because he was related to the young man by marriage he deemed it dishonourable to deliver him up to his death. At last, after many days of discussion, a treaty of lasting friendship was agreed, which they preferred to call a truce for a period of years. Among other clauses in this treaty or truce, the most important clause was that James should expel Peter Warbeck from his kingdom.

> *Polydore Vergil **The Anglica Historia 1485–1537***

◢ Document D

(1499) This was the end of Peter Warbeck, who despised his humble origin, and by twisting falsehood into truth, truth into falsehood, deceived many, including men of considerable standing, until at last he fell upon the scaffold, victim of his own deceit. Then, a few days afterwards, Edward Earl of Warwick was himself beheaded. The entire population mourned the death of the handsome youth. Why indeed the unhappy boy should have been committed to prison not for any fault of his own but only because of his family's offences, why he was retained so long in prison, and what, lastly, the worthy youth could have done in prison which could merit his death – all these things could obviously not be comprehended by many. But truly the wretched lot of the Yorkist house was such that Earl Edward had to perish in this fashion in order that there should be no surviving male heir to his family.

> *Polydore Vergil **The Anglica Historia 1485–1537***

TASKS

◢ Document E

Now it has pleased God that all should be thoroughly and duly purged and cleansed, so that not a doubtful drop of royal blood remains in this kingdom except the true blood of the King and Queen and above all that of the lord Prince Arthur.

Letter from the Spanish envoy, de Puebla, to Ferdinand and Isabella, 11 January 1500

a Explain the following references:

  i 'a feigned boy, surmising him to have been the son of the Duke of Clarence' (Document A lines 2–3)   *2 marks*

  ii 'anxious to make a marriage alliance with him' (Document C lines 4–5)   *1 mark*

  iii 'because he was related to the young man by marriage' (Document C lines 9–10)   *2 marks*

b In the light of the Document E, comment on the reasons for the mission of Pedro de Ayala to Scotland (Document C).   *4 marks*

c 'He was dangerous only because of his persistence and because of the willingness of other rulers to use him to embarrass the King of England.' Show how far these documents support this verdict on Perkin Warbeck.   *8 marks*

d What evidence is there in these documents and any others known to you that Polydore Vergil was correct in his explanation of the reasons for the execution of the Earl of Warwick (Document D)?   *8 marks*

Question **a**: These are questions of fact, designed to see if you can work out what the sources are 'getting at'. For (i) you need to show that you know that they are referring to Simnel, and the clue is that it goes on to talk about another 'lad'. Note the use of the word 'feigned' which you came across in *The Book of Houth* extract. (ii) simply checks that you know that the suggested marriage is that of Arthur to Catherine. (iii) asks you to write about the marriage between Warbeck and Lady Catherine Gordon, James IV's cousin.

Question **b** refers you to the Spanish connection again, and some of the marks will be given for a reference to Ferdinand's need for an English alliance against France (about which you will know more when you have studied Henry's foreign policy in Chapter 5). Also, of course, the monarchs needed to be sure that Henry was really secure on his throne before committing their daughter to his son. You have time to add a little about the normal, unfriendly relationships between Scotland and England, and to mention the later English/Scottish marriage alliance. If you know that Pedro de Ayala was one of the most trusted envoys of the Spanish Crown, then you can make the point that this was a high profile mission.

For **c** make sure you understand the question, so that you can mentally divide your answer, looking at 'his persistence' and 'the willingness of other rulers to use him …' separately. Try to find evidence from each of the sources: document **A** shows you all the different places he tried; **b** shows you his considerable military strength and so on. Similarly, Documents **A**, **B** and **C** give you most information about the foreign help and support Warbeck obtained. The third ingredient of a question containing the word 'only' is to consider whether there were any other features which made him dangerous. There are references in both **D** and **E** to the threat of the Yorkist supporters, so you may decide to refer briefly to this aspect.

Question **d**: It is probably worth paraphrasing Vergil's comments. The question may say 'reasons' but Vergil in fact only gives one. This question gives you a chance to sum up Henry's situation in 1499: how secure he was, what other threats there were to him, and so on. It also allows you to show your knowledge by pointing out that there still were some male Yorkists alive – the de la Poles for instance – but they were not nearly as directly in line to the throne. Vergil sketches briefly the fate of Warwick since 1485, and you could expand on that, pointing out that a 24-year-old was more dangerous than the 10-year-old originally imprisoned in 1485. Finally, Vergil clearly did not think the boy had 'done in prison' anything 'which could merit his death' so you need to explain what the excuse was which led to his execution and how valid an excuse it was. A further reference to the foreign policy connections as a reason for the death would round off your answer.

Some source-based questions include a secondary source. A useful exercise would be to select a paragraph about the pretenders from a modern historian (the final paragraph of this chapter, for instance) and make a comparison between the statements it makes and the evidence you have in the other sources in the question.

TASKS

Answering examination essay questions

It is worth taking every chance you can to practise essay questions, particularly if you attempt them in the time allowed (which varies from module to module and from board to board), so that you get into the habit of planning efficiently and writing relevantly. Examiners dislike most the kind of answer which appears totally to ignore the particular question they have set. They like best a logical line of argument, backed up by accurate factual evidence.

How serious was the threat posed to Henry VII by pretenders to the throne?

Your plan should focus on the key words in the title: the thinking you have done about the ingredients needed to make a rebellion successful will help.

One possible structure might be:

1 Introduction: discussing the extent to which Henry was vulnerable to attacks from opposition groups. You need also to define the word 'pretender'. It is interesting to note that this doesn't literally mean someone who 'dresses up as' someone else; its original reading was someone with pretensions to a particular position.

2 The Simnel threat and what made it serious, or not: the foreign connections; the situation in England; Henry's limited dynastic security at the time. Then you should discuss the ease with which Simnel was defeated.

3 A similar paragraph on Warbeck, especially picking out the differences: the timing; the help received abroad; the links with other trouble in England.

4 A summary paragraph, discussing whether there was any real danger from either of these pretenders, and what ingredients could have made them more dangerous, leading you to point 5.

5 A brief discussion of the other problems which posed a threat to Henry: the need for security in his family; foreign problems and risks; the hostility and dangerous nature of the baronial class. You will want to link these to the pretenders, with examples of which foreign powers and English nobles were supporting Simnel or Warbeck. Also the equation of shortage of money against popular resistance to taxation, seen most clearly in the Cornish rising.

6 It should then be possible to reach a conclusion about the pretenders: a serious threat? compared to other threats? in the light of Henry's insecure situation? Was one of them more of a serious threat than the other?

Key ingredients for a successful rebellion (from task 1, page 47)

◢ A possible replacement ruler who would be accepted by the people who matter.

◢ Support from the barons, or at least a substantial group of them.

◢ Significant backing from abroad.

◢ Armed force adequate to win battles.

◢ Approval of the Church.

◢ Discontent with the existing state of affairs among both ordinary people and the important groups.

From task on page 21

Why do kings do as they do?	What constraints force them to behave properly?
glory?	perceptions of God?
security?	sense of duty?
duty to their people?	foreign threats?
duty to God?	fear of the nobles? the masses?
family obligations?	
the need to pay back favours?	
fear of some group or groups?	

CHAPTER THREE

WAS THE COUNTRY 'WELL GOVERNED' DURING THE REIGN OF HENRY VII?

Objectives

◢ To investigate what 'good governance' meant in the late fifteenth century, and what the obligations of the king were seen to be

◢ To study the strategies used by Henry to tackle the problem of public order and to curb the independence of the nobility

◢ To look at the mechanisms used by Henry in his government and to see the extent to which they were 'medieval' or 'modern'. Were they new, or the same systems as had been used by earlier kings?

◢ To decide which criteria we should use to judge Henry's success in government, and to reach conclusions about his achievements.

Before you can decide whether England was well governed, you need to know what the government was expected to do. To clarify this, try task 1 on page 77 now.

You will notice how much more we require of our governments nowadays: health, social welfare, education, roads, the proper upbringing of children, control of racial attitudes, defence, consumer protection and so on. Similarly, modern governments expect to work through an elected parliament, with publicity for legislation both before and after it is issued.

Henry VII had less to do than modern governments; but at the same time he was responsible in person for much more of the day-to-day running of the country: he had assistants, but he chose them himself. In the end, the country was his to run and to control. Keep this contrast in mind: it will help you to avoid anachronisms in your own thinking.

'The nation state'

Historians of early modern Europe describe this as the period when 'the nation state' developed. They regard the nation state as one symptom of the Renaissance, and point to the ending of feudal loyalty to the overlord, replaced by loyalty to the national king. Contemporary political thinkers and writers were intent on glorifying the status of the monarch, and discussing the ways in which a ruler could do the best for his country. Britain, because of its island geography, has always had more of an identity than the populations within the shifting borders of central Europe; by Henry's reign, England had only small possessions in France (the March of Calais) and the national identity was strengthening. Another issue worth bearing in mind as you study Henry's methods of governing is the extent to which they follow the patterns of the rest of Europe: a comparison with the countries you will be looking at in Chapter 5 will be useful.

Henry's view of monarchy

At the end of Part 1, you considered the motives of monarchs in the late Middle Ages; this Chapter should help you to see why and how Henry operated as king. His obligations were clear:

- ◢ to protect his people from dangers, both external and internal;
- ◢ to ensure they were able to lead good, Christian lives;
- ◢ to establish and maintain a balance between the different social classes and groups.

He had been chosen by God to do this, and he had the right to collect contributions from his people to enable him to carry out his duties. His reputation throughout Europe and his own kingdom was that he was wise, and that he was not interested in flattery. He took time and care over his government, a fact which is especially noticeable if we compare him to his son, Henry VIII, particularly at the carefree start of his reign. M. Alexander (*The First of the Tudors*, 1980) comments that 'personal monarchy', a term often applied to Henry, means especially his conscientious attitude and approach to ruling. While this showed most in his scrupulous handling of the finances, it is also clear that he kept a firm eye on all aspects of his government.

Henry's methods

Neville Williams (*The Life and Times of Henry VII*, Weidenfeld and Nicolson, 1973) wrote that Henry was 'essentially medieval in outlook … his role was much more that of the last of the medieval kings than that of the first "modern" monarch of England'. We need to consider the mechanisms of government normally used, and see whether Henry ruled in the same ways as his predecessors or was an innovator.

For Henry to maintain the security of his kingdom and his people, he needed both to make use of, and to control, the most powerful class in England: the nobility.

The nobility

Nobles were traditionally supposed to be the lieutenants of the king, though during the Middle Ages they had as often been his opponents. About 25 per cent of lords had fought against Henry at Bosworth and many others had stayed neutral. But many of the opposing barons had been killed or captured in the battle so there was less opposition. Henry needed the nobles to keep secure the various parts of the country and he relied, having no choice, on old nobles like the Percys and the Howards, even if he did not trust them.

Earlier monarchs had been inclined to ennoble their own supporters, but all titles were hereditary, and so Henry faced various noble families who owed their titles to the Yorkists. Henry did not make a lot of new nobles. In all, he ennobled nine men – seven of them in the first three years, 1485–8. One purpose of this (according to J. R. Lander) was to bring useful people into parliament.

Henry had also knighted 11 loyal men on the field at Bosworth, which made them eligible to stand for the House of Commons in the shires. In addition, as previous kings had done, he used the Order of the Garter as a reward or form of patronage, making 37 new Knights of the Garter during his reign.

Nobles normally controlled substantial areas of land, often with a castle or fortified house as a base. While the development of guns had made castles less formidable than they used to be, they remained the focus of local power; Henry knew the dangers of this kind of local power. The castles of the Crown, together with those confiscated from

Yorkist sympathisers, were put into the hands of members of his Household, rather than being allocated to new nobles, or to the families which had others nearby.

Retaining

What made the barons particularly dangerous was the practice of retaining, which was defined in Part 1 (page 13). Henry was determined to end the menace once and for all. This was complicated by the fact that Henry needed the retainers of his own supporters to maintain law and order, and to form the nucleus of a national army in case of war. It was standard practice for the Crown to license other people's retainers 'for the king's service'. (This required the king's signature together with either the *signet* or *privy seal*.)

KEY TERMS

Signet and **privy seal**: the use of seals is thought to date from the period when kings and most of the people likely to be receiving their instructions were illiterate. By the end of the fifteenth century, the Great Seal was a way of formalising government orders, and the different seals were used for the king's own orders and instructions; his private, or privy seal, and his signet, which, as you can see from the name, was a substitute for his signature. The Lord Chancellor could only use the Great Seal with permission via the privy seal, which in turn had to be warranted by the signet. By this time, both had offices of the Household attached to them, which carried out the various instructions of the king.

Nowadays there is a Government Officer, the Lord Privy Seal, whose function is mainly to be the Leader of the House of Lords for the government. The seal itself is no longer a significant part of government!

Edward IV's parliament had passed laws against retaining (1468). Laws of Henry's reign effectively renewed and extended these, as particular difficulties were identified. In 1502, a law banned all retainers in the counties of Kent and Sussex, though a few licences exist which show he made exceptions where he trusted the barons concerned. The 1504 Statute of Liveries ordered all trials concerning illegal retaining to be conducted in London only, in the *prerogative* courts. Every person who kept retainers was required to give a list of their names to the king and to obtain a licence from him. The purpose of this was to limit the risk of maintenance and embracery, that is attempts by nobles to influence or intimidate judges and juries.

KEY TERM

Prerogative means the rights that a ruler has by virtue of his or her position (literally, from the Latin, the rights exist before they are asked for). Thus the prerogative courts are the courts that the king sets up to administer his law, rather than the common law of the land.

These laws did not end retaining. Nobles were of course allowed to employ people with specific functions, like grooms, guards and so on. So some families such as the Percys duplicated estate and household roles to increase the number of purposeful and therefore legal retainers. However, Henry did reduce the numbers of retainers whose function was only to fight if called upon, and the control of the issue of liveries reduced the risks of public disorder when retainers of two rival factions met in the street. Indeed, there were times when the retainers might be summoned, with their lords, to serve the king.

Attainders and bonds and recognisances

Another way of controlling the barons was to threaten them with terrible consequences if they were disloyal. Kings had always used **_attainders_**, but Henry was more moderate than some of his predecessors.

Henry issued 138 acts of attainder in his whole reign, which may seem high until we remember that he had come to the throne by war and had faced several serious rebellions. Twenty-eight of these date from 1485, and a further, similar, number from the Battle of Stoke and the end of the Simnel rebellion. Some of the early attainders were actually posthumous (for example that of John Duke of Norfolk) to make it possible to seize the family property. Twenty of the attainders of 1485 had been reversed by 1495 and two more by the end of the reign, so only six actually stood. Most of the reversals were partial, however, with some of the property kept back, or with substantial financial inducements to the King. Some were restored in full, but only in stages, for instance to the Duke of Norfolk's heir, the Earl of Surrey.

Henry probably preferred to use **_bonds and recognisances_**, 'a second, almost equally terrifying system of control' (Lander). Huge sums were payable in instalments and often with land held by the king as security until the payments were complete: whole families faced total ruin if one of their members misbehaved. For example, on

22 May 1491, 55 people were 'mainprized', or held liable, for the good behaviour of Thomas Marquis of Dorset. These ranged from the Earl of Kent at £1,000 to a mercer called Thomas Quadryng who was liable for £50. The list includes bishops, priors, knights and merchants. These bonds seem particularly terrible to a modern student but, as Lander says, how else was a king to control 'such a mob of aloof, self-interested magnates'? The bonds probably ensured fewer executions and imprisonments than in previous and subsequent reigns, but the arbitrary and heavy-handed nature with which they were used made them particularly unpopular.

When he inherited his father's throne, Henry VIII recognised how much antagonism the bonds and recognisances had bred. He used his father's ministers, Richard Empson and Edmund Dudley, as scapegoats: they were accused of corrupt practices in assessing and collecting money. Dudley's defence that he had only carried out the King's express purpose did not save him. Henry VIII was thus able to gain popularity by ending nearly two hundred recognisances, admitting that many had been wrongly extorted.

KEY TERMS

Attainder means declaring a person to be a traitor, often by Act of Parliament rather than through a court of law. Because the family of the traitor is 'tainted', that is, poisoned, by his or her treason, the entire property of the family is forfeited to the Crown. It is quicker than the due process of law, and gives the supposed traitor little chance to make his or her version of events known.

Bonds and recognisances: these two terms are used interchangeably in documents from the period, and indeed, by modern historians. In theory, a bond was a written commitment to perform some specific action, and to pay a sum of money if that action was not performed; a recognisance was a formal acknowledgement of an obligation which already existed. What both meant in practice was that large sums of money were held by the king to ensure good behaviour. The money would belong to the king if the noble, or the person he was 'insuring', went against the government. Many of the noble families found them crippling.

◢ Primary source

Here is an example of a bond of recognisance from 1505 (Calendar of the Close Rolls (3) Vol. II no. 499), which shows the King using the recognisance as an attempt to control the wild behaviour of retainers:

... for £2,000 by Henry, Lord Clifford. Condition: Henry to keep the peace for himself and his servants, tenants and 'part-takers' [that is, those who side with him or take his part], *especially towards Roger Tempest of Broughton, and endeavour to bring before the King and his Council within 40 days such of his servants as were present at the late pulling down of Roger's place and house at Broughton.*

The King's Council

Henry's main instrument of government was his Council, which included nobles, but also included people from other groups, so that the nobles had no chance of dominating. The Royal Council advised the King on everything, and he was almost always at Council meetings, but the decisions were his and not theirs.

Here are some figures which show the make-up of the Council:

> For the whole reign of Henry VII, 227 councillors are known, though at each meeting there would be 20 or fewer in attendance. Members of the royal family would attend from time to time.
> 43 were peers
> 61 were clergy of one kind or another
> 49 were bureaucrats, government officials
> 45 were regular attenders at court, who were not nobles but knights or members of the gentry
> 27 were lawyers: these were important as they decided if what the King wanted was legal, i.e. constitutional, or not. One example of their importance is when Henry wanted to issue attainders without consent of parliament and they declared this to be unlawful. (Thus, as A. F. Pollard suggested in *The Evolution of Parliament*, 1926, these Council lawyers acted in the same way as the Supreme Court of the USA does.)

> Several of these councillors already had experience of government: 16 had been councillors of Edward IV, 19 had been Richard III's councillors, and 13 of these had been both. In addition, 15 more had been related to Edward, which perhaps shows Henry's tolerance, or at least his recognition, of the need to keep the Yorkists involved.

⬛ The Council included an 'inner ring' which met more frequently: a key figure of this inner circle was John Morton – Lord Chancellor, Archbishop of Canterbury in 1487, Cardinal in 1493 – who can be described as Prime, or at least Chief, Minister until his death in 1500.

At first, the Council travelled with the King, meeting wherever he was, but in 1497 a Lord President of the Council was appointed for when the King was away on a progress or on a diplomatic or military expedition. As this President was never someone who headed a department of the government, there was no risk that he would take over too much power. The Council met at the King's will. There were usually various items to discuss, and the King would listen to the views or advice of members before coming to his decisions. It is clear that the Council organised the wording of statutes to be put before parliament, and councillors had considerable influence in both Houses of Parliament. The King's Council also played a considerable part in the judicial system, which will be discussed later in this chapter.

Local government: the Sheriffs and the Justices of the Peace

Over the centuries, kings had appointed various officials to try to reduce the power of the nobility in their home areas. An important royal official in each county was the Shire Reeve, or Sheriff. These men administered the king's laws and kept his peace. Sheriffs supervised the muster of the militia, organised other aspects of local life and were closely involved in the pursuit and trial of major criminals. They could demand the attendance of selected local people – whether as a jury or as a panel of enquiry – when local knowledge would be very valuable in achieving justice. Justices of the Peace (JPs) worked closely with the local administration of their areas and were increasingly relied upon during the Tudor period.

Henry VII took an interest in appointments and their duties were increased all the time, usually through parliamentary statutes: 21 statutes were passed during Henry's reign concerning the position and duties of JPs. While it is hard to demonstrate whether or not they were efficient, it seems likely that Henry found them useful, since otherwise he would not have increased their responsibilities. They are often used as an example of Henry's growing reliance upon the middle classes rather than the nobility. JPs also administered the king's justice at the community level, and ordinary people were more likely to come into contact with them than with any other part of the royal judicial system.

The judicial system

The king was regarded as the chief justice of the kingdom; he appointed and supervised royal judges and JPs; his judges travelled the country 'on circuit'. Henry was anxious that all his subjects should obtain proper justice. In 1495, for example, he ordered that poor men should be given free legal aid, so that they could have their cases heard and receive justice. It is probably useful to have an overview of the whole judicial system before we consider what use Henry made of it in the administration of the country.

Local courts

There were many courts at the community level: borough, manorial and guild courts were not really the concern of the king, any more than the Church courts were. These local courts were, however, concerned with local and specialised matters only, and most serious cases would be heard by royal judges. Most cases were heard at either the county courts, presided over by the Sheriffs, or the quarter sessions, presided over by JPs. Twice a year, royal judges 'on circuit' held the assizes and heard both serious criminal cases and civil cases sent back from the central courts in order to benefit from local juries and advisers with relevant knowledge. The most important courts outside London were, by this time, directly in the hands of the Crown. These were the courts of the Marches of Wales, the County Palatine of Chester and the Duchy of Lancaster, now part of the royal system.

Central courts

At Westminster, there were many courts, some of which were entirely specialised, for example the Court of the Exchequer, dealing with cases arising from revenue collection, and the Admiralty Court, dealing with maritime cases. Other courts administered either common law or equity. Common law was the customary law of England, unwritten, but based on the centuries of judgements given by previous royal judges. The courts of King's Bench and Common Pleas were common law courts, the first dealing with appeals from criminal cases in local courts, as well as civil cases, especially trespass. Common Pleas heard cases connected with civil affairs such as land conveyancing and debt. The common law had become very cumbersome and slow: before a plaintiff could begin an action, he or she had to purchase a writ, the form of which would be in Latin and dated from the reign of Edward I. Any minor inaccuracy in the wording of a writ could cause delays. Proceedings and judgements were in Norman French. It is not surprising that, by the reign of Henry VII, plaintiffs preferred to have t heir cases heard by an equity court, such as the Court of Chancery, where proceedings were in English, and where the principles of conscience, fair conduct and natural justice were paramount. The reign of Henry VII saw a significant increase of cases being heard in Chancery, a continuing trend from the Yorkist period. The Court of Chancery officially acknowledged commercial transactions and 'uses' (trusts for the ownership of land, designed to keep the property out of wardship). Unlike the Court of Common Pleas, Chancery was responsive to the needs of people at the time, such as the growing number of merchants.

The Council as a law court

Equity was also used in the various courts based on the King's Council. Concern for poor men's causes was expressed by the Council, and lesser members of the Council sometimes heard such cases. Subsequently, in the reign of Henry VIII, the Court of Requests for Poor Men's Causes emerged as a more or less independent body. Members of the Council also sat to do justice on a regular basis. Cases were heard 'upon bill or information' and in fact virtually all the cases dealt with in Henry VII's reign were between party and party, and not prosecutions initiated by the Crown. Of the cases dealt with in Henry's reign, only about 10 per cent were criminal. Otherwise the Council dealt with embezzlement, fraud, defamation and land disputes. It also looked into issues like complaints against sheriffs, or attacks on municipal rights. The purpose of all this (as Roger Lockyer and Andrew Thrush note) may have been to ensure that the Council took a lead in preventing violence, but it simply overburdened the Council with civil actions. These are cases which, in modern Britain, we usually leave to the Ombudsman and other regulatory bodies. In 1487 and 1495 Henry organised conciliar tribunals to deal with perversion of justice and perjury in lawsuits heard in other courts.

The 'Council Learned in the Law' was the name given to meetings of a small number of councillors, dealing particularly with cases involving the rights of the Crown's lands, revenue collection and the king's debts. The Council Learned is known to have been in operation by 1495 and became independent of the King's Council. It emerged as the instrument of royal extortion and, as such, had a poor reputation, to say the least. It was involved in the process of issuing bonds and recognisances, and the councillors had considerable scope to fix the penalties of those found to have infringed the law. Henry VII's minister, Dudley (in the Tower in 1509) wrote a list of 84 cases where the King had used accusations from dishonest people 'on very light ground' or 'on the surmise of a lewd fellow' to have people arrested or threatened, or both, because they were seen as dangerous.

The fact that the King's Council, in its judicial function, met in the chamber with the star-painted ceiling has led to some confusion with the later prerogative Court of Star Chamber, which was to used as an instrument of royal control by the Stuarts and was finally abolished in 1641. In fact, the purpose of the Act of Parliament of 1487, misleadingly known as the Star Chamber Act, was to set up a specialist tribunal to deal with the particular issue of liveried retainers. The Chancellor, Treasurer and Keeper of the Privy Seal, or any two of them, plus a bishop and a temporal lord from the Council were to meet as a court and deal with issues of retaining, livery and maintenance. Records of only 10 cases heard before the tribunal survive.

Henry used the law courts in a variety of ways as an important part of his strategy for keeping the kingdom at peace. His justice was wide-ranging and, until the later years of his reign, perceived as fair. His revenues benefited from the fines collected by the courts. It is clear, however, that Henry could be unscrupulous when it suited him, even in the field of justice.

The Church

Henry was not able to organise a complete and uniform system of justice, however, since the ***Church courts*** and the ***benefit of clergy*** still existed. Some of the senior Church courts, including those of the diocese of Durham and Abbeys of Peterborough, St Edmunds and St Albans were now under Crown control, but the Church still controlled most of its own judicial system.

KEY TERMS

Church courts were law courts in the control of the Church, to hear cases involving canon, or Church law. They dealt mostly with clerics who, when accused of crimes, had the benefit of being tried by Church court; however, they also dealt with lay people who had broken canon law, even if they had not broken the law of the land.

Benefit of clergy: the right of clerics to have cases against them heard in the Church courts, where punishments were limited to fines, imprisonment or excommunication, rather than the more violent punishments of the secular courts. The system was corrupt, because the proof needed before a man could be tried in the Church court was simply to recite the 53rd Psalm, the 'Miserere.'

Henry's son and successor was to remove the separate jurisdiction of the Church, but only as part of the much greater upheaval of the Reformation.

The Church as an instrument of control

Henry, in common with many of his contemporary rulers, recognised the Church's important role in maintaining social stability and in ensuring people's loyalty. Kings of England nominated bishops, who were then installed by papal decree. As you will see in Chapter 4, the finances of the Church were of considerable interest to the King, as well. At a time when education was controlled by the Church, and most educated men were clerics, many churchmen served the King in his government. Oliver King, who was Henry's secretary, became Bishop of Exeter, and then Bishop of Bath and Wells. (It was he who rebuilt the Church of Bath Abbey, which had fallen into decline, and was responsible for the carving of Jacob's Ladder on the West Front.) Similarly, Bishop Morton was the Lord Chancellor and then Archbishop of Canterbury; Richard Fox, Lord Privy Seal, became Bishop of Exeter.

Henry, like other European rulers at the time, was aware of concerns about the state of the Church. His sympathy with reformist ideas can be seen in his appointment of the scholar John Colet as Dean of St Paul's, and his parliament ordered bishops to supervise carefully the morals of their clergy. Henry was always prepared to deal with **heresy** when it arose, although there were few burnings in his reign. He also, as we have seen, ended the right of sanctuary in cases of capital offences; in this, as in other issues, he ensured that he retained the support of the Pope.

KEY TERM

Heresy: a heretic is someone who claims to be a Christian while failing to accept some or all of the teachings of the Catholic Church. In the fifteenth century, the largest group of heretics in England were the Lollards, followers of John Wyclif who believed, among other ideas, that the bible and Church services should be in English, and that clergy should live in poverty as Christ did. Naturally, the official Church dealt fiercely with heretics, excommunicating them and then handing them over to the state to be burned alive, a foretaste of what would happen to their souls in hell.

Henry appears to have been aware of both the strengths and weaknesses of the Church. Its firm hold on the minds and spirits of the people was of use to him. On the other hand, his attempts to reform the various abuses would be popular with people who resented the extreme wealth and occasional misbehaviour of some churchmen. Henry's own devotion to the Christian faith can be seen both in his church building and in his foundation of Franciscan observant houses at Richmond and Greenwich.

The government of Ireland

Ireland was nominally ruled by the Crown of England. The Irish lords had, however, taken advantage of the Wars of the Roses to shake off English control, and Henry was shown how dangerous this could be by the Simnel rebellion. It was partly because of this that, in September 1494, Sir Edward Poynings was made Lord Deputy of Ireland. The series of laws which he introduced brought Ireland more closely under control.

Poynings' laws: a summary

- Parliament in Ireland could only meet and legislate with prior permission of the king and Council and the Lord Deputy.
- All laws of the English parliament were to apply to Ireland too.
- The Court of Castle Chamber was to meet under the presidentship of the Lord Deputy to deal with knotty problems.
- An Act of Resumption was issued for all crown land alienated since 1327 (which was the end of the reign of Edward II).
- A 5 per cent duty to be paid to the king was imposed on all imports.

The effectiveness of these new laws, and of Poynings' deputyship was confirmed when the Irish lords refused the opportunities offered by Perkin Warbeck's rebellion. Ireland was to remain comparatively quiet until the end of the next century.

Government in Wales and the North

Wales never posed a major problem for Henry VII. Partly because of his family links, Wales itself was always fairly peaceful. The Welsh Marches had been areas of disorder, but Edward IV had improved the situation by absorbing or annexing 23 Marcher Lordships for the Crown, and setting up the Council which Henry then renewed. He made a point of appointing Welshmen, not only in Wales but in other key positions as well. The Council of Wales and the Marches had, nominally, at its head Arthur, who from the age of 10 was in Ludlow learning how to be a king by ruling Wales, with expert guidance from his uncle, Jasper Tudor. When Arthur died, Henry took several months before naming his other son as Prince of Wales, and never let him go to the Marches. This was partly because of his anxieties about the health of his last surviving son, but also because neither the Marches nor Wales was causing any problems. In 1493, the Council was given judicial powers (Henry VIII was to enhance the powers of the Council, and Buckingham's rebellion in 1521 gave him the excuse to take over the crown for the last few Marcher lordships).

In the North, the situation was both better and worse than in Wales. The form which trouble might take was more predictable there than in

Figure 6 Arthur, Prince of Wales, from a stained glass window in Malvern Priory

the unreconstructed Welsh Marches. On the other hand, it was further away from the centre of government. It was more lawless and so did need control; and there was no core of loyalty to Henry. Richard III had set up a Council in the North under John de la Pole, Earl of Lincoln, to undercut the power of the Earl of Northumberland. The changing allegiances after the Battle of Bosworth made things difficult, but various nobles were given special authority to ensure that no single family gained too much power.

The dangers of the area were confirmed in April 1489, when the Earl of

Northumberland was murdered by anti-tax rioters in Yorkshire. The fragility of control was demonstrated since he was there for the King supervising the collection of the subsidy. Henry did not establish a conciliar structure like that of Wales, though his son was to do that. He found after the problems of the 1480s that he was able to maintain control without formal structures. Henry also had the advantage that the quarrels with Scotland meant that the northern lords were inclined to remain loyal to England.

Defence

An important function of the government was of course the defence of the realm. There was no standing army, because of the cost, although there were a few full-time paid garrisons. These were at Carlisle and Berwick to guard against the Scots, and Calais, Guisnes and Hammes, in the March of Calais, to protect England's last continental possessions. Instead, England was defended by the militia. Males aged 16–60 had the customary duty to keep suitable arms and be ready for muster by constables. The militia was armed with bill and bow – that is a spear-type implement like a long-handled pruning knife – and a longbow. These were still effective, in a period when guns were very new indeed and only a few were hand-held.

The Commissions of Array then selected those needed and collected money instead from those not selected. Selection was often done according to the geographical position of the problem the force was due to tackle, in order to minimise travel and rural dislocation. Male citizens had other obligations. They were required to run the coastal beacons, and to watch on the coast. Northern militias had similar duties on the Scottish border. They could, in addition, be asked to 'follow the fray', that is, to assist their neighbours in case of crime.

This military system was not strong. For example, the Cornish rebels in 1497 got all the way to Blackheath, south-east of London, before they were stopped. Even in foreign wars, England's military force was limited. When Henry VII invaded France with 12,000 men in 1492, this force was less than half the size of each of the other major European powers. We can see that any opposition group which had got together a huge army could obviously have toppled Henry. The fact that they did not is evidence of the efficiency of Henry's government.

Parliament

Parliament was used as part of the king's government. You read an outline summary in Part 1. This chapter explains the part played by parliament in greater detail. Later centuries were to see conflicts between Crown and parliament, resulting in victory for the House of Commons, but at this stage parliament was simply a tool of the administration. Although Henry did not call parliaments frequently, or allow them to last long, he made substantial use of the passing of statutes: 192 Acts were passed during Henry's reign, an average of 27 statutes per parliament. (There is a list of the main statutes passed, at the end of this section.) Twenty-one of these laws were about JPs; nine dealt with common law procedures; seven concerned changes in land law. Often, though, the 'law and order' Acts were of limited duration. They were frequently only to last until the next parliament met.

The King had a great deal of control over parliament, and his servants were active in the Commons, which met within the precincts of Westminster Abbey. The King's own ministers, like Richard Empson and Edmund Dudley, were both MPs, and in fact both had been Speaker briefly. The job of Speaker was hard work, and not one which ordinary Commons members wanted. The MPs were happy to have one of the King's men filling the position and dealing with the resultant administration. During Henry's reign there was virtually no opposition from parliament, although there was a little friction about feudal aids in 1504.

◢ Primary source

Who (Thomas More), ere ever he had been reader in Court [i.e. a lecturer at the Inns of Court], *was in the latter time of King Henry VII made a burgess of the parliament wherein they were by the King demanded – as I have heard reported – about three-fifteenths for the marriage of his eldest daughter that then should be the Scottish queen; at the last debating whereof he made such arguments and reasons there against, that the King's demands thereby were clean overthrown. So that one of the King's Privy Chamber, named Master Tyler, being present thereat brought word to the King out of the parliament house that a beardless boy had disappointed all his purpose. Whereupon the king, conceiving great indignation towards him, could not be satisfied until he had some way revenged it. And forasmuch as he, nothing having, nothing could lose, His Grace devised a causeless quarrel against his father, keeping him in the Tower until he had made him pay to him an hundred pounds fine.*

From William Roper, More's son-in-law **The Life of Sir Thomas More** (first published 1555)

This story shows us that Henry liked to keep firm control over the Commons, and was prepared to take action to ensure that there was no opposition. Mostly, however, parliament worked without conflict, and much was achieved as you can see from the following.

Henry VII's parliaments: a summary

First: 7 November 1485

Main developments included:
- Of the 29 secular peers summoned to the Lords, only 18 attended.
- Thomas Lovell, Treasurer of the Chamber, was elected Speaker.
- The Act of Settlement announced that Henry was King, without going into details about how or by what right. His reign was dated from 21 August 1485 (i.e. the day before Bosworth).
- The revenues from customs duties were voted to the King for life, though he had not asked for them.
- The Court of Requests was abolished by petition of the parliament (though it was soon to be restored).
- Act of Resumptions allowed the King to take back Crown lands lost since October 1455. (This was made less effective by the fact that 461 properties were excluded; but was a signal to barons not to expect grants of Crown land in the future.)
- 28 people were attainted, including several, like Richard III, who were already dead. (All but 8 of these were to be reversed by 1495.)
- Parliament reminded the King of his promise to marry Elizabeth of York.

Second: 9 November 1487
- Two-tenths and two-fifteenths were voted (defined in Chapter 4).

◢ 28 of the rebel leaders involved in the Battle of Stoke and events leading up to it were attainted.

◢ A new Tribunal was set up: the Lord Chancellor, Lord Treasurer, Lord Privy Seal, two Chief Justices, two peers, one temporal and one spiritual. This soon came to be known as the Court of Star Chamber.

Third: 13 January 1489

◢ The purpose of this parliament was to obtain money for foreign policy; after serious disputes, £100,000 was agreed.

◢ A statute ensured that the king (as overlord) had the right of wardship over minors, even if the parent had tried to set up a family trust to avoid this.

◢ An Act in Restraint of Sheep Farming (against enclosures, mainly because of anxiety about depopulation in coastal areas).

◢ Wool to be exported only under licence (by the Company of Merchants of the Staple at Calais).

◢ Regulations to assist poor people in getting justice without cost.

◢ A Private Member's Act ordered English merchants to use English ships for their exports.

Fourth: 17 October 1491

◢ Two-tenths and two-fifteenths were granted, after warnings by the Commons that it might be hard to collect.

◢ A Private Member's Act tried to standardise Weights and Measures.

Fifth: October 1495

◢ De Facto Act: there was to be no punishment for obeying the reigning king, even if he was subsequently overthrown.

◢ The king was encouraged to collect the arrears of the tax grant from 1491.

◢ Parliament suggested that the maintenance of Berwick Castle should be at the charge of the people of the North.

◢ The duties of JPs were elaborated and increased.

◢ A statute provided for free justice in certain circumstances for the poor.

Sixth: January 1497

◢ Two-tenths and two-fifteenths were agreed (total £120,000) at the same time as Convocation (the assembly of the Church) voted money.

⊿ JPs were to help appoint and assist Royal Tax Collectors, and to supervise them and report misconduct.

Seventh: January 1504 and lasting nine weeks

⊿ JPs were given the job of looking into the use of debased coinage, and reporting failure to accept money at face value.

⊿ JPs were ordered to control riotous behaviour in their areas.

⊿ Statute of Liveries, which mainly restated a statute of 1468, imposed high fines for liveries; JPs were to report infringements to the Council or the Court of King's Bench.

⊿ The King demanded feudal aids for the marriage of his daughter and knighthood of Arthur; opposition in Commons was led by the 26-year-old Thomas More, but in the end, Henry got £31,000.

⊿ 51 attainders issued.

The use of the House of Commons is one aspect of Henry's wish to find alternatives to the nobles. R. H. Tawney wrote as long ago as 1942 that Henry 'courted the middle class' (*Harrington's interpretation of his Age*, London, British Academy). This was not only in the Commons, however, but also as sheriffs, as JPs and as 'civil servants' in the various offices of his administration. Of course, as explained in Part 1, the term 'middle class' means rural gentry as much as it means town dwellers, bankers, merchants and so on. The distinction between town and country was less clear then than it is now, since many wealthy townspeople acquired estates and titles. This meant that his patronage became an important part of the king's range of power tools. There was a growing spectrum of people who were influencing, and were influenced by, the Crown.

Summary

How well did Henry govern? If you compare the situation before and after his reign you have to say that he had done well. Law and order was established; the budget was in surplus, as we shall see in Chapter 4; trade was flourishing, and with it the merchant classes; nobles were no longer a danger to national order; the Church was less corrupt than it had been, though still far from perfect; ordinary people could be confident that their lives would not be disrupted by the kind of disorder which their forefathers had suffered.

Henry's own aims, if we assume that they were to maintain peace and security and to ensure a smooth inheritance to his son, had been amply fulfilled.

1 Discuss in pairs what modern governments do. Make a list of duties and obligations. Then identify any which also applied in the late Middle Ages.

2 A useful way to make notes from this chapter would be to create a summary diagram, showing all the different groups and institutions which the King made use of, and how they were connected to one another and to him.

3 Look back at the section on page 66. Does the fact that Dudley was trying to please the new King, and save himself from execution, make his evidence less reliable?

4 You may find it useful to research and make separate notes on Ireland under the Tudors as a development theme.

5 Was Henry VII medieval or modern? Chapter 6 will give you a chance to consider this question, and to look at the views of different historians on the subject. For the moment, you will find it helpful to go through and summarise Henry's methods. Identify which appear to be completely new, which were adopted from earlier kings, and which were Henry's adapted versions of earlier methods. This exercise will provide you with examples to back up or question the various opinions about Henry's government.

Examination practice

This is a 'document question' from the University of Cambridge Local Examinations Syndicate, which shows you how clearly you need to know and understand the mechanisms of Henry VII's government. As was suggested in Chapter 2, make sure that you are being relevant in what you write, and match the amount you write to the number of marks available for each part question.

When you have thought through what the answers should be, have a look at the notes and comments at the end of this chapter.

◢ Document A

And after dinner, all the justices were at Blackfriars to discuss the King's business for the parliament. And several good statutes were mentioned, very advantageous for the Kingdom if they could be carried out. These were the statutes compiled in the time of

Edward IV ..., viz. Winchester and Westminster, for robberies and felonies, the statute of riots, routs and forcible entry, the statute of labourers and vagabonds, of tokens and liveries, maintenance and embracery ... But the question was, would they be carried out? And the Chief Justice said that the law would never be carried out properly until the Lords spiritual and temporal are of one mind for the love and fear they have of God, or the King, or both, to carry them out effectively.

A Law Report, 1485

◢ Document B

The King our Sovereign lord remembereth how by unlawful maintenances, giving of liveries, signs and tokens, and retainers by indenture, promises, oaths, writing or otherwise; embraceries of his subjects, untrue demeanings of sheriffs in making of panels, and other untrue returns; by taking of money by juries, by great riots and unlawful assemblies; the policy and good rule of this realm is almost subdued ... Be it therefore ordained that the Chancellor and Treasurer of England for the time being and Keeper of the King's Privy Seal, or two of them, calling to him a bishop and a temporal lord of the King's most honourable Council, and the two Chief Justices of the King's Bench and Common Pleas for the time being, or two other justices in their absence, upon bill or information put to the said Chancellor, for the King or any other, against any person for any misbehaving afore rehearsed, have authority to call before them by writ or privy seal the said misdoers, and them and others by their discretions, to whom the truth may be known, to examine; and such as they find therein defective, to punish them after their demerits, after the form and effect of statutes thereof made, in like manner and form as they should and ought to be punished, if they were thereof convicted after the due order of the law.

The 'Star Chamber' Act, 1487

◢ Document C

The King enacteth, ... that no person ... give any livery or sign to retain any person, other than such as he giveth household wages unto without fraud or colour, or that he be his manual servant ..., by any writing, oath, promise, livery, sign, badge, token or in any other manner wise unlawfully retain; and if any do the contrary, that then he run and fall in the pain and forfeiture for every such livery and sign, badge or token so accepted, 100 shillings [£5], and the taker or acceptor of every such livery, badge, token, or sign, to forfeit ... 100 shillings.

Moreover the King our sovereign lord ... hath ordained ... that every person that will *sue or complain before the Chancellor of England or the Keeper of the King's Great Seal in the star chamber or before the King in his Bench or before the King and his Council attending upon his most royal person ... against any person or persons offending or doing against the form of this ordinance ... be admitted by their discretion to give information ... And the said Chancellor or Keeper of the seal or the King in his Bench the said Council to have power to examine all persons defendants and every one of them, as well by oath as otherwise, and to adjudge him or them convict or attaint ... in such penalties as is aforesaid as the case shall require; ... and also the same party plaintiff or informer shall have ... reasonable reward ...*

And also it is enacted ... that the said Chancellor or Keeper of the great seal, justices, or Council have full authority and power by this statute to do send by writ, subpoena, privy seal, warrant or otherwise by their discretion, for any person or persons offending ... without any suit or information made or put before them ...

The Statute of Liveries, 1504

a Explain the following references:
   i 'liveries' (Document A line 6)   *1 mark*
   ii 'embracery' (Document A line 6)   *1 mark*
   iii 'maintenances' (Document B line 1)   *1 mark*
   iv 'untrue demeanings of sheriffs in making of panels' (Document B lines 3–4)   *1 mark*

b What does Document B tell us about Henry VII's response to the comments of the justices in Document A?   *6 marks*

c To what extent does a comparison of Document B and Document C suggest that there had been a significant advance in Henry VII's attitude towards the problem of retaining?   *7 marks*

d 'The problems of disorder in Henry VII's reign required not so much new laws as the enforcement of those which already existed.' Examine this assertion in the light of these documents and of any others known to you.   *8 marks*

Question **a**: These are simply matters of definition, and you should be able to explain quite crisply what the terms mean. (iv) You need to know that 'demeaning' means 'humbling' or 'insulting' but the other two key words (panel and sheriff) should be known to you.

Question **b**: For six marks, it is worth being very specific! If you go through Document A and pick out all the problems which the justices list which are then addressed by the so-called Star Chamber Act, you will have the framework of a good answer. The need for the 'fear ... of the King' is dealt with by the fact that it is the king's own mechanisms which are to deal with the threats of danger.

Question **c**: Again, a close comparison between the two documents is called for. You need to comment, with examples, on the increased precision of Document C; the punishments are spelled out, as are the offences. The most substantial change, however, is the provision for anonymous, and well-rewarded, informers, and for compulsion when it comes to court attendance. It is also worth noting that the 1504 statute punishes receivers of liveries, the retainers themselves, rather than just the lord.

Question **d**: There are references to earlier statutes directly in Document 1, and indirectly in the other two, and these should form the central part of your answer. You will gain some credit for explaining briefly why the earlier laws had not been fully enforced, and for noticing that the court which met in the Star Chamber had become a settled part of the structure between 1487 and 1504. If you want to disagree with the statement, some examples of law and order problems which could not be handled by the existing laws would back up your point. If you have read other contemporary sources, you need to refer to some of them: the references in Polydore Vergil about the King adopting the legislation of Edward IV, or references to bonds, recognisances and attainders as the main instruments against disorder among the higher classes.

CHAPTER FOUR

WHY AND HOW DID HENRY ACHIEVE FINANCIAL AND ECONOMIC SECURITY FOR HIS CROWN AND HIS COUNTRY?

Objectives

◢ To study the ways in which Henry used custom and traditional financial practice to extend the resources of the Crown

◢ To decide whether Henry was unnecessarily grasping, and whether he exerted unfair pressure on his subjects in his financial demands

◢ To decide how successful Henry was in encouraging the development of English commerce and trade

◢ To consider what the financial motives of the Crown were

◢ To reach conclusions about Henry's impact on the domestic economy.

Where did the money come from?

The theory of government finance in the later Middle Ages bore little relationship to what actually happened. The king was supposed to 'live of his own', that is, to pay for the government of the country out of his own private revenues. The theory was based on the idea that the kingdom belonged to the king, so it was up to him to cover its running costs. In practice, by this time, the costs of government had grown so much that it was recognised that the king had to have help from the country when he was doing things for the good of the country. Sir John Fortescue, in the 1470s, had referred to the 'exquisite' or exceptional means that the king might use to raise the money he needed for the increasingly complex business of government. Customary revenues remained the most important, however, and some of them are identified below.

Customary revenues
Crown land

The king, like any landowner, collected rents from his land. This was about 35 per cent of ordinary revenue, but Henry increased rents during his reign by 200 per cent. This meant that the income, which in 1485 was £12,000, had risen to £41,000 by 1509. This increase was helped by the growth in the amount of crown land there was. The King gained some because of attainders, and more by inheritance and through **reversion**. Unlike his predecessors, the King rarely re-allocated land to new noble families, preferring to have it administered by his own agents.

Feudal wardship

Wardships were very profitable and one of the few new offices which Henry established was that of Master of Wards (1503). An overlord was entitled to administer the orphan's lands, during his minority, to his own advantage, and Henry used and abused this right. He was, for example, allowed to organise the marriages of female orphans and of the widows of his vassals. He made new laws to prevent families setting up trusts which would mean that wardship was not needed. The amount netted in wardships went up from £350 per year at the start of the reign to £5,000 in 1505 and £6,000 by the end of the reign.

> ## KEY TERMS
>
> **Reversion**: in feudalism, the king was the overlord and gave out land to his tenants, or vassals. If the family died out, the land naturally reverted to the king.
>
> **Wardship**: as overlord, the king also had the duty to care for the under-age children of dead tenants, and to look after their land until the heir reached an age to be able to fulfil his duties as vassal in return for use of the land.

Other applications of feudalism

From December 1486 Henry sorted and checked tenancy agreements, ensuring that as many landholdings as possible were held directly from him (that is *in capite* or 'in Chief'), so all the wardships and other feudal obligations were due to him and not to any other lord. Similarly, where there were sub-tenancies, Henry made sure that he did not sacrifice too much revenue.

Henry seized every opportunity to collect feudal money. Although it was within his rights as a landlord to do so, these specific feudal aids may be seen as 'extraordinary'. An overlord had the right to demand money on special occasions from his vassals: Henry collected the payments due when his oldest daughter was married, and when his oldest son was knighted. This money was not collected until after Arthur's death, however, which is an indication of Henry's willingness to get the most from his feudal rights.

The customary income from these and other sources was supposed to cover household food, clothes, wages, buildings, furnishings and all the king needed from day to day. It was also meant to provide for annuities and presents and all buildings, including defences built in peacetime. Even embassies and peacetime diplomacy were meant to be paid for out of ordinary revenue. Any abnormal expenditure, such as defence or war, was to be paid for by the people. In fact, though, customary expenditure was getting too high to be covered by normal revenues, so other sources were being collected regularly and used even in peacetime. Some historians regard these revenues as 'customary' since they were collected every year. You will find that the different books you read categorise them in different ways; all you need do is be sure you know whether the king collected the money as his personal right, or by authority of some other part of his administration, such as parliament or the law courts. Some of his sources of 'extra' revenue are outlined below.

Extraordinary revenues

◢ **Customs duties on imports and exports**. Some of the customs duties were the king's by prerogative, and some historians regard them as customary revenue for that reason; but he was also given the right to collect other sums by Parliament. The tradition was that the first Parliament of each reign would authorise their collection. (In 1625, the refusal of Charles I's Parliament to do so was a first sign of the hostility which was to end in the Civil War.) The most important customs revenues came from tunnage on imported wine, and poundage on exported wool and various other commodities. Because Henry VII did so much to encourage trade, by the end of the reign, the customs were one of the principal sources of the royal income. The importance of this revenue helps to explain why JPs in coastal areas were ordered to deal fiercely with smugglers. Henry was, of course, also using trade as an instrument of foreign policy (you will read more about this later in this chapter). It would be hard to say which was more important to him: diplomacy for trade, or trade as an instrument of foreign policy?

Subsidies might be voted by Parliament for specific needs. At the start of Henry VII's reign, these were the ancient 'one-tenth and one-fifteenth', usually voted two at a time, with a date by which they should be collected. The tenth was on movable property in the towns; the fifteenth, movable property in the countryside. The valuations of property had been fixed county by county some decades before. One result was that they were not as productive as they should have been, and Henry ordered new valuations to be made. These revised subsidy valuations were just about ready as Henry VII died, so his son reaped the benefit. Parliament voted a total of six subsidies during his reign, but we must not think this was entirely straightforward. Professor J. R. Lander states that there was always a problem, which was that Henry could not risk imposing too much direct taxation, much less risk reforming the existing tax system so that it 'bit' better, in fear of alienating the nobles, who, after all, sat in the Lords.

You have seen examples of resentment about the collection of taxation actually leading to rebellion. The vote of two-fifteenths and two-tenths from all, and further 'aid' of two more of each from the rich in January 1497 was what sparked off the troubles in Cornwall. In the North, tax riots culminated in the murder of the Earl of Northumberland. Nevertheless, the subsidies were a key part of the King's income. M. Alexander calculates that throughout his reign Henry raised a total of £281,999.

Proceeds from Justice were a source of revenue, though of course this was a bit unpredictable (the fines, bonds and recognisances were discussed in Chapter 3). Henry also received gifts and annuities from people involved in Star Chamber cases if the cases turned out right for them.

Towards the end of the reign Empson and Dudley chased after debtors and collected sureties and bonds previously owed to other creditors, with the Council Learned in the Law headed by Richard Empson from 1505 to enforce their collection.

◢ **Interest-free loans and benevolences** (gifts) were often very unpopular and resented. Henry always repaid what he borrowed, however, so his credit was good when it mattered. For instance, the Corporation of the City of London lent large sums of money without complaint: in 1487 £4,000, in 1488 £2,000 and in 1490 £2,000. Other 'gifts', or benevolences, brought in £48,000 for the war against France. It could perhaps be argued that benevolences at least came from the wealthy, rather than from the taxpayers as a whole. As time went on, and Henry's other sources of income were established, borrowing of this kind became less necessary.

◢ In October 1496 a special assembly of notables, the last meeting of the Great Council of earlier reigns, agreed to a new benevolence in the face of the Scottish threat over Warbeck: but it did not raise as much as it should have, which demonstrates that the King was not willing to press too hard for money at this stage.

◢ Henry sometimes sold offices in his household or government, or at least accepted presents from newly appointed people!

◢ **The Church** offered money through *Convocation*, which usually met at the same time as parliament. In 1487 and 1496, the Church offered one-tenth of the assessed valuation of all *benefices*. This was quite valuable because the Church did the collection for the king. There was no question of rebellion, since the Church was able to threaten eternal punishment for those who disobeyed. In addition, there was quite a lot of royal *simony* such as the gifts of £1,000 for appointing a Dean of York and £300 for an Archdeacon of Buckingham. The king was also entitled to the income from vacant dioceses. In 1492, for example, Henry got £1,800 while Bath and Wells was vacant. The king gained another sum when a new bishop was appointed, since he was entitled to First Fruits: one-third of revenue in the first year of a new bishop. This is probably why Henry moved his bishops about so much, though some people have suggested it was about control and preventing prelates acquiring local power bases. Some estimates (for instance, J. J. Scarisbrick in the *Journal of English History* Vol. XI, 1960) suggest that the income from the Church between 1485 and 1547 averaged £12,500 per year, though of course that average also includes the fruits of Henry VIII's Reformation, so Henry VII's income would have been less.

KEY TERMS

Convocation is the assembly of the Church in England, consisting of representatives of each diocese and religious order.

Benefice: any position in the Church from cardinal down to sexton or gravedigger.

Simony is the term used for the purchase or sale of benefices. The word comes from the story of Simon (Acts of the Apostles 8:18–21) who offered the disciples money to be taught how to heal the sick as they did.

Commerce and trade

As we have seen, Henry collected the customs duties on imports and exports. He was aware of the benefits of increasing trade to the wealth of the whole country, and throughout his reign he made treaties which enhanced trade opportunities, even if their main purpose was more directly diplomatic.

In 1489, two agreements were signed with direct relevance to trade opportunities. The renewal of the century-old Lancastrian friendship treaty with Portugal included specific trade commitments. Another treaty, with the Hanseatic League of German towns, which dominated trade in northern Europe, gave England trading rights in Denmark and at Bergen in Norway, as well as fishing rights in Icelandic waters.

Henry's treaty-making was not always successful, however. In 1490, a treaty was signed with the Medici family who ruled the state of Florence, permitting the English wool traders to set up a staple, or base, in Pisa. This resulted in a tariff 'war' with Venice, which harmed England. Since at this time oriental goods such as spices and silks were transmitted to England by Venetian merchants in the so-called Flanders Galleys, any dispute with Venice was bound to affect adversely the supply of luxury items to England. The French invasion of Italy in 1494 put an end to disputes like this one.

It was more common for Henry to 'win' diplomatic encounters. One benefit of the Treaty of Etaples of 1492 was to ensure that trade with France was not interrupted. Burgundy's support for Perkin Warbeck led to an embargo on trade with the Netherlands from 1493 to 1496. This was ended by the favourable *Intercursus Magnus* trade treaty, which confirmed the rights of English merchants in Antwerp. A commercial treaty in 1497 formed part of Henry's negotiations with Charles VIII of France, and in 1506, Henry seized the opportunity to sign a trade treaty when Philip of Burgundy and Joanna of Castile were forced by storms into an English harbour.

Henry's concern for trade can be seen in other ways too. In 1497, legislation standardised weights and measures, although local variations remained. He also provided bounties for people who built merchant ships, and gave tax credits for ships purchased abroad. A dry dock, for ship repairs, was built at Portsmouth in 1495–96.

Opportunities for trade were, of course, growing fast, and Henry took an interest in the new geographical discoveries. He did not sponsor Christopher Columbus, though the explorer's brother did visit England and ask him for backing. Four years later, however, he listened with interest to the Venetian, John Cabot, and paid some of the costs of the voyages which took Cabot to the coast of North America, probably the St Lawrence estuary. Henry's account books record gifts made to the travellers who returned from the new-found land. Had Henry VIII been as interested as his father, England might have been a major player in North America a hundred years before the Pilgrim Fathers.

These are by no means all the ways in which Henry enhanced the revenue of his kingdom. After all, the marriage of his son to the Aragonese princess, Catherine, brought him a substantial dowry. These examples do show, however, that Henry was adept at making money, and that revenue was always one of the considerations in all aspects of his policies.

His various methods were certainly successful. At the start of the reign, in 1485, the annual income of the Crown was £52,000, of which £20,000 came from the customs duties. By 1509, the total had risen to £113,000 a year, and the share derived from customs, while it had risen to £40,000, was playing a smaller part. From 1492, Henry was in credit at the end of every year.

How was the money administered?

The Exchequer was the traditional institution of finance, but it was very slow and inefficient. In theory, it tallied and accounted for all income and expenditure. Sheriffs were required to attend and hand over revenues from their counties, and state officials requested funds for their various needs. The Yorkist kings had begun to bypass the Exchequer by using the Chamber of the Household, and Henry now did the same. The Household's function was to supply the material needs of the king and all those who lived or stayed at court, but the Officers of the Household tended to overlap with the Officers of State, since they were people who were always with the king. The Chamber was more flexible than the Exchequer, and more willing to use modern accounting methods. Henry was able to check the accounts, and page after page bear his annotations and initials. At first the Chamber dealt with 'new' revenues such as the proceeds from confiscated estates, and gradually it took over more and more sources of income. By 1489, the Chamber was handling 25 per cent of revenue, and by 1509, 90 per cent of ordinary revenue was dealt with by the Household. The key figure behind these changes, and the increased efficiency which resulted, was Sir Reginald Bray. In September 1485, Henry appointed him as Chancellor of the Duchy of Lancaster, but in practice, his role could be described as 'Minister in Charge of Money', and Henry trusted him.

The king's personal funds were in the charge of the Privy Chamber, formerly the Groom of the Stool. Henry tended to keep his money in the Jewel House behind his bedchamber.

How did Henry spend his money?

The King was interested in building, both for his own pleasure and for other motives. He paid for the chapel of King's College in Cambridge to be finished. As well as the glory of God, this of course reflected the veneration of Henry VI to which Henry was committed. When Sheen Palace burned down, he replaced it by having Richmond Palace built, with no expense spared (1497–1501). Then, in 1502, he began the extension to Westminster Abbey where he was eventually buried.

Henry was aware of the propaganda value of magnificent state occasions, and he spent large sums on the christenings and later the

Figure 7 An engraving of the procession to the baptism of Arthur, eldest son of Henry VII

marriages of his children. Here is an account of the baptism of Arthur, from which we can see both the lavish expenditure and also the participation of members of many noble families.

◢ Source

Lady Cecil, the Queen's eldest sister, bore the Prince, wrapped in a mantle of crimson cloth of gold furred with ermine with a train which was borne by My Lady the Marquis of Dorset, and Sir John Cheyney supported the middle of the same, the Lord Edward Widevill, the Lord La Warre, the son and heir of the Lord Audley, and Sir John Arundel bore the canopy.

*From Leland **De rebus Britannicus collectanea** (1487)*

Henry was also very interested in culture: he bought a great many books of both writing and music for himself. Thomas Linacre, internationally famous for his medical research, and founder of the Royal College of Physicians, was his personal physician and Prince Arthur's tutor. The Dutch philosopher and writer, Desiderius Erasmus, was welcomed, making a total of six visits to England, the first in 1498. From 1501 onwards, Polydore Vergil, a historian and writer from Urbino, lived in England under the King's sponsorship. John Skelton, the poet, worked for Henry from 1488. Bernard André, a poet from the south of France, was welcomed and designated Royal Tutor and Poet Laureate.

Henry also encouraged printing, though there was no official printer for the King until 1504. By 1501, William Caxton's successor, Wynkin de Worde, published 110 books with an average print run of 500 copies each. There were six printers working in England by 1500 (according to H. S. Bennett, *English Books and Readers 1475–1557*, CUP, 1970). Items printed included Henry and Elizabeth's marriage Papal Bull, also his right to the throne. Such information was made into printed bills to be posted. Later, other pamphlets were printed, such as the 1508 arguments in favour of Princess Mary marrying Charles of Spain.

The willingness of Henry to invest in printing can be interpreted in various ways: was he aware of the value of printed propaganda as the number of literate people in the country increased? Or was he merely concerned to promote the cultural life of his country to match that of the continent?

His account books also show him gambling, paying for court entertainments and rewarding people who amused or pleased him.

The King allocated money from the first to the Yeomen of the Guard (50 at first but by 1500 there were 200 of them). From 1500 on, £1,200 per year was set aside for their pay and their upkeep. He also invested money in the navy. By 1509, although there were only seven men-of-war, they were of good quality and very well armed.

Conclusion

When Henry died, he left £9,100. (A way of realising how much this was is to bear in mind that a carpenter earned 40d, or one-sixth of a pound, per week.) His will included instructions for 10,000 masses to be said for his soul at 6d each, as well as £2,000 for the sick and needy and £5,000 for King's College Cambridge. His preference for Cambridge may be explained by the fact that Oxford was still inclined to support the Yorkists, and by its connections with the 'sainted' Henry VI, last of the Lancastrian kings, martyred by the Yorkists. As well as safeguarding his own soul, Henry VII had ensured the financial security of his realm and his son, and had established mechanisms which were to be adapted and adopted by his successors.

TASK

Class discussion on the motivation behind Henry's financial policies

Having studied the text on Henry's financial and economic policies, you will realise that there is still a certain amount of controversy concerning Henry's motives and the manner in which he pursued his financial interests. As a class activity, discuss Henry's motives by carrying out a ranking and prioritising exercise. Study the assorted motives below:

- To ensure the effectiveness of defences against foreign threats by being able to employ soldiers directly.

- To fund such a substantial 'standing army' that no individual or group would risk rebellion.

- To enable Henry to indulge in his own pleasures, such as gambling, music and fine clothes.

- To ensure for Henry's soul a smooth passage through purgatory by enabling him to give substantial sums to the Church.

- In order to display his power in a lavish, generous court to impress foreign diplomats and enhance his prestige.

- To enable him to pursue his chosen policies without being forced to obtain the cooperation of parliament.

- To impoverish the barons so that they were not in a position to pose a threat.

- To avoid punitive tax levels which might upset the common people (as happened in Cornwall).

- To secure his dynasty by establishing a strong financial base for the future.

- To widen the gulf between the king and his noble subjects and thus protect and enhance his status.

- As a side-effect of his policies on law and order, to ensure a reputation of mercy while still bringing the nobles under control.

- To entangle the nobility in a financial web of bonds and recognisances so that they could not even contemplate independent action.

With a partner, pick the nine motives which you regard as most important: you may find you want to group some of them together, if you think they overlap. Then make a diamond, like the one shown here. This would mean placing the most important motive at the top of the diamond and the least important at the bottom.

motive 1

motive 2   motive 3

motive 4   motive 5   motive 6

motive 7   motive 8

motive 9

Or you might decide that building a pyramid is more appropriate in showing the motivation behind Henry's policies. This would involve putting the most important aim at the tip and working down to the least important towards the base of four motives.

This exercise should give you the opportunity to discuss some possible motivations which influenced Henry's financial policies and to clarify your own understanding of why he pursued particular actions.

Writing an essay

Assess the success of Henry VII in strengthening the financial position of the Crown.

This is a typical essay question on this topic. In organising your information for such an essay, you need to make some clear notes of your own and evaluate policy used to generate royal income. This will also help you to see what additional reading you need to do. You might find it useful to organise your ideas in a table like the one below. You will first need to discuss how you will judge effectiveness of each source of revenue. Remember to consider whether the revenues were 'customary', 'extraordinary' or on the border between the two.

Source of income, or revenue-raising strategy	Details, explaining what the revenue was and how it was collected	Effectiveness of policy
Crown lands		
Customs duties		

Revenue raised through the operations of the judicial system		
Parliamentary grants		
Loans and benevolences		
Bonds and recognisances		
Feudal obligations		
Clerical dues and other income from the Church		

Once you have a clear understanding of all the different sources of revenue, you can tackle the essay. The big risk, as you will have noticed, is that it could easily degenerate into a list, rather than keeping to the point, which is HOW SUCCESSFUL it all was. A useful introduction might be to comment, using your Diamond 9 exercise, on how success might have been measured, by Henry, or by other contemporaries. You might also discuss what other motives Henry had, so that success in finance was not the only criterion. One way to evaluate success might be to discuss opposition or lack of it; another might be to see whether the systems were used more than once. Decide on a structure which keeps the reader interested in what you are saying, and then use the detailed examples to back up an argument.

It is worth getting to know this topic well, and reading more about it, since it is seen as one of the key topics in the study of Henry VII.

CHAPTER FIVE

HOW DID HENRY'S RELATIONS WITH FOREIGN POWERS HELP TO SECURE HIS DYNASTY?

Objectives

⊿ To understand Henry's motives in his relations with foreign powers

⊿ To examine the methods he adopted and judge his effectiveness in securing his aims.

Before you take an in-depth look at Henry's policies you will need to know a little about Western Europe at the time of Henry's accession. Try task 1 on page 110.

Henry's situation in 1485

Henry's interactions with foreign powers were shaped by his principal aim: the need to secure his crown and his dynasty. In order to ensure stability, and to protect his position, removing domestic threats to the throne was essential. You will find studying Henry's relations with foreign countries inextricably linked with events surrounding the pretenders (discussed in Chapter 2). You will have noted that rival claimants to the throne tried to further their interests by gaining support from foreign powers, leaving Henry to react to the threat of invasion. Strengthening the Crown financially was also vital and Henry knew that costly engagements with foreign armies had to be avoided. Hence Henry pursued a defensive foreign policy. That is, his main aim was to protect his existing position and possessions by seeking to get the better of other powers.

Henry was no doubt aware of his incredible achievement in winning the crown and, although he was never timid, he had realistic ambitions for English influence on the continent. He wanted to be fully involved in European affairs: he did not isolate himself from developments on the mainland. Having spent 14 years in exile in Brittany and France, he was perhaps more continental in outlook than

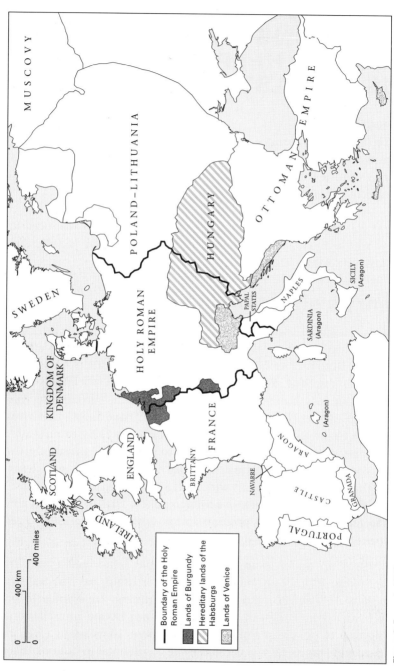

Figure 8 Europe in 1485

preceding monarchs. Polydore Vergil, who provides a remarkably balanced description of the character of Henry VII, notes that 'he was fond of having foreigners at his court and he freely conferred favours on them'. Having secured the throne he personally only returned to the continent once, crossing the Channel to lead an English army against France in October 1492. Instead, Henry skilfully cultivated links with the courts of European monarchs through the development of *diplomacy*.

KEY TERM

Diplomacy is the process of communication and negotiation in relations between states, by peaceful means. This activity is conducted by officials, such as ambassadors or envoys, who rely on tact and discretion to promote the interests of their own country, while retaining the goodwill of the host nation. The practice of diplomacy grew considerably in the late fifteenth century. Henry VII appointed permanent ambassadors to foreign courts. They kept Henry well briefed on the local situation, by relying on information gleaned from a variety of sources, including direct audiences with foreign rulers. Intelligence was also gathered by more underhand methods, for example, using paid informants and spies.

Despite the growth of more efficient communications between courts, there is no doubt that Henry took personal responsibility for overall strategy in his relations with other countries. His main interest was foreign policy and he would have learnt a lot in exile from observing at court the negotiations for treaties and marriage alliances.

Ferdinand of Aragon was already involved in developing new diplomatic methods and, particularly in the early years of the reign, Henry took advantage of a strong relationship with Spain, exploiting Spain's established diplomatic and intelligence networks. Doctor De Puebla, the Spanish ambassador at the English court, appears to have won the confidence and favour of Henry – and the two men talked freely. One of the successful results of Henry's diplomacy were the marriage alliances negotiated with other monarchs. These were an important way of building up the strength, respect and prestige of the Tudor dynasty. Overall, Henry's approach was sensible but largely unglamorous.

It is convenient to outline the foreign policy developments of the reign in a broad chronological survey. While reading the narrative do not forget to bear in mind the objectives listed at the beginning of the chapter.

1485–87

Henry acted immediately to neutralise any potential foreign threats to his position as monarch. The prompt measures he implemented were designed to buy him time and avoid any unnecessary risks. The land border with Scotland was a perennial problem, which could easily be exploited by opponents. Henry skilfully reduced tensions with Scotland, taking advantage of the limited backing the Scottish Crown had given Henry at Bosworth. Peace with Scotland was secured in a three-year truce, which was signed between Henry and James III in July 1486. The likelihood of Scotland interfering in English politics for its own advantage was further reduced in 1488 when James IV, aged 15, succeeded to the throne following his father's death.

It was even more important for Henry to secure French acceptance of his position as king. Henry played on the backing that the French had given him in his campaign to win the throne in 1485. Henry did not preoccupy himself with the facts of England's historic enmity with France. Instead he signed a one-year truce with France which was later lengthened to last until January 1489. Henry's realism is reflected in the fact that he astutely kept quiet about the traditional claims of English kings to the throne of France, although he certainly did not appear to be weakly submitting to the French. Henry was also lucky that the Regency government of France was preoccupied with domestic affairs as restive nobles were involved in rebellion. Henry also sensibly used his personal links with Brittany to reach agreement on a commercial treaty with Francis II in 1486. It subsequently proved more difficult for Henry to maintain useful ties with France and Brittany after the death of Francis II in September 1488, as you will see below.

Diplomatic relations were also established quickly with other key rulers. These included the rulers of Spain: Isabella of Castile and Ferdinand of Aragon. Henry first dabbled in the game of royal marriage bargaining as early as 1487, when his son Arthur was not yet one and Catherine, daughter of the Spanish monarchs, was less than two! In the short term the more experienced Ferdinand remained wary of moving too quickly. In his view England was a relatively minor power and the dynastic basis of the new Tudor monarchy still looked rather precarious. However, the very fact that negotiations were taking place proved to Henry that he was being taken seriously and being accepted on the continent as ruler of England.

Henry found relations with Burgundy were more problematic although the country was traditionally England's ally against France. The presence of Margaret, Duchess of Burgundy, was a significant factor in how relations evolved with England. (You can look back to Chapter 1 to remind yourself of her relationship with the Yorkist kings, Edward IV and Richard III.) Margaret had derived her title through her marriage to Charles the Bold, Duke of Burgundy, who died in 1477. Traditionally Margaret has been portrayed as a dominant figure, bearing 'great malice' against Henry VII and constantly involved in Yorkist intrigues through family loyalty. Her exact motivation is unclear, but she must, as Henry himself acknowledged, have been aware of the responsibility of Richard III for the downfall of the Yorkist dynasty. The current ruler of Burgundy was Maximilian Habsburg of Austria. He was Duke because of his marriage to Mary of Burgundy, daughter and heiress of Charles the Bold. Maximilian played a part in shaping Anglo-Burgundian relations. He was fearful of Henry's more positive relations with France and perhaps felt that the truce signed with France threatened Burgundian interests. Ultimately, Maximilian was preoccupied with threats to his Austrian Habsburg lands and lacked the power to contain the independent actions of Margaret.

Burgundy became a haven for Yorkist exiles and their intriguing. As you have already seen, Margaret of Burgundy was involved with the Lambert Simnel conspiracy of 1487. Despite Henry's victory over the Yorkist pretender at the Battle of Stoke, the episode emphasised his continued vulnerability and the need to be ever vigilant in keeping a check on the activities at the courts of neighbouring powers. Burgundy was a vital commercial ally for England, as the port of Antwerp was the main centre for the export of English woollen cloth, but Henry was prepared to sacrifice the interests of trade if his dynasty was threatened.

1487–93

English foreign policy in this period was dominated by French determination to annex Brittany. Henry showed his inherent caution and realism in his handling of the crisis between France and Brittany which flared up quickly after the success at Stoke. He was forced to react to circumstances, pursuing a practicable course rather than getting sucked into to unsustainable military conflict. He was acutely aware of the limited nature of the resources available to the English Crown for overseas campaigning.

Henry VII wanted to avoid offending Brittany or France for as long as possible and in 1487 he did not get drawn into taking a partisan position. However, ultimately the end of an independent Brittany would threaten English security. Its strategically significant coastline was an important buffer, protecting England from the threat of a French invasion. Alienating France was still too risky: the French court could become the focus for another claimant to the throne, threatening Henry's dynastic security.

Lacking any official foreign support, Francis II was defeated by the French in July 1488. Crucially, in the subsequent treaty agreed with France, Francis was forced to agree that any marriage for his daughters could not proceed without the authorisation of the French King. The crisis escalated with the death of Francis II in September. His 12-year-old daughter, Anne, inherited the Duchy. The French Regent, Anne of Beaujeu, was determined to annex Brittany and used feudal law to claim wardship of the child Duchess Anne of Brittany. Henry VII was now forced to respond actively and although he was still wary of alienating the French he signed the Treaty of Redon with Brittany in February 1489. You will see how its main terms reflect Henry's inherent caution and financial restraint:

◢ English agreement to support Brittany in its attempt to maintain independence;
◢ Brittany would bear the expense of an English expeditionary force of 6,000 English troops.

Henry worked quickly to ensure that the now overt alliance with Brittany did not leave England isolated and vulnerable to French attack. He successfully concluded separate agreements with Maximilian and Ferdinand. The Treaty of Medina del Campo was concluded with Spain in March 1489. It was an agreement:

◢ that neither side would harbour or support each other's rebels;
◢ that both states would assist each other in defending their lands against any enemy whatsoever;
◢ to reduce customs duties between the two countries, to the mutual advantage of their trade;
◢ that neither side would assist France or sign an alliance or treaty with France without the agreement of the other;
◢ that betrothal negotiations for the eventual marriage of Arthur and Catherine would proceed.

It was a triumph for Henry and was a culmination of the tricky diplomatic negotiations for a royal marriage referred to earlier. Henry VII had to put up with a few frosty comments from Ferdinand along the way, but the Treaty was certainly a high point for English diplomacy. It marked Henry's arrival as a player of status on the European stage and further cemented the survival chances of the Tudor dynasty. Spain was now blocked to potential Yorkist claimants. The Treaty benefited Ferdinand as there was a long-standing dispute between France and Aragon over two border provinces, Cerdagne and Rousillon. Ferdinand's aim was to regain these territories, occupied by France since 1462.

Henry was less successful in protecting the independence of Brittany. By April 1489 English troops did go into action in Brittany but the support of its allies was minimal. Spain was preoccupied with the reconquest of Granada and Maximilian found himself overstretched in trying to defend Austrian Habsburg lands. In 1490 Maximilian tried to halt the tightening French grip over Brittany, by marrying Anne of Brittany by proxy. This was not legally binding and only Maximilian's physical appearance or military action could have been effective. In the end Brittany had no choice but to accept defeat and in December 1491 Anne was married to Charles VIII of France. Brittany was now incorporated into the territorial possessions of the French Crown.

The loss of Brittany presented Henry with the most challenging foreign policy problem of his reign. Not only was English security threatened by complete French control of the Channel coastline, but the untimely emergence of a new pretender, Perkin Warbeck, was compounding his difficulties. Claiming to be Richard of York, Warbeck had arrived in Ireland in the autumn of 1491. Evidence from Warbeck's confession made before his execution suggests that Charles VIII was involved with Warbeck from the early stages, saying 'The French King sent an ambassador into Ireland ... to advertise me to come into France ...'. It would certainly have suited Charles to use Warbeck as a bargaining chip in future negotiations with Henry.

Henry acted decisively. He set the ball rolling to raise cash for action against France. Parliament was summoned in October 1491, agreeing to a grant for the campaign. Henry's action reflects his ***pragmatism***. He could not have ignored Brittany and weakly accepted French control, despite his vulnerable situation. Henry VII was well aware of the humiliating defeats Henry VI had faced at the hands of the French. He also knew his own position as monarch would become unsafe if he quietly endorsed the French achievement. On the other hand, he had no unrealistic dreams of destroying the power of the French Crown or recreating an English empire in France. Henry invaded France, landing in Calais in October 1492. The fact that he left it so late in the campaigning seasons is definite proof that his intentions were limited from the start. English resources would never have sustained prolonged action against the French. Henry besieged Boulogne and this was enough to bring Charles VIII to negotiate with the English. Charles was a very different character to Henry. His head was full of chivalric notions and as a romantic idealist he was in search of military glory, not against the English, but in Italy.

KEY TERM

Pragmatism: historians use this word as shorthand to explain policies which are adopted, or practical actions which are taken, to suit the problems and situations of the moment. This is in contrast to policies which are part of a carefully planned strategy or following a set of ideals.

Agreement was promptly reached and the Treaty of Etaples was signed in November 1492. Charles VIII agreed to these main terms:

◢ to withdraw aid to all Yorkist claimants and rebels against the Tudor dynasty (obviously including Warbeck);

- ◢ to make up back payments for Edward IV's pension, agreed by the earlier Treaty of Picquigny (1475) – meaning in fact that Henry himself became a French pensioner;
- ◢ to cover the costs of Henry's military intervention in Brittany.

The Treaty of Etaples was an unglamorous, but practical, agreement for Henry. There could be no great victory celebrations since Brittany was still lost to France. However, Henry had not formally withdrawn the English claim to the throne of France and had derived some financial benefit from the campaign. Vergil provides a contemporary interpretation of Henry's possible motivation:

◢ Source

Henry, a man in general of the most prudent disposition, did not fear the enemy, to whose forces his own were not unequal; nor did he aim to secure cash, but was rather actuated by a desire for honour and for his own safety. For it was at this time that he learnt that Margaret, widow of Charles, Duke of Burgundy, had raised from the dead one of the sons of King Edward, her brother, a youth by the name of Richard; and that this youth was with Charles to persuade the French King to supply him with arms against Henry.

Polydore Vergil ***The Anglica Historia***

Early reactions to the Treaty of Etaples from other powers were not favourable. Spain was not fully consulted as it should have been, but by 1493 relations between Ferdinand and Henry were back on a more positive footing. This was because Charles VIII had reached a separate agreement with Ferdinand, returning the territories of Cerdagne and Rouisillon to Aragon. Maximilian was also put out and felt that he had been deserted by Henry in 1492. Crucially, Maximilian appeared to react by condoning Margaret of Burgundy's decision to harbour Warbeck when he was forced to leave France. In retaliation Henry set up a trade embargo against Burgundy in 1493, rerouting the export of woollen cloth to Calais. The resulting counter-blockade benefited no one and this episode only serves to emphasise that Henry always saw it as necessary to put Crown security before commercial gain.

1493–1502

In this period Henry VII was able to exploit his skills and become a more significant player in the field of European diplomacy. England itself had not become stronger economically, but Henry had achieved the recognition he desired and was seen as a useful ally against the growing power of France. At first Henry was still preoccupied with the threat to his security from the Pretender, Warbeck. He felt threatened as long as foreign powers were prepared to meddle in English domestic affairs, supporting the Yorkist cause for their own advantage.

Anglo-Scottish relations remained strained as long as there was support for Warbeck in Scotland. Diplomatic channels between the two countries stayed open and the breakthrough appeared to come in 1495 when negotiations for a marriage between Henry's daughter, Margaret, and James IV of Scotland were first suggested. The situation soon deteriorated when Warbeck fled Ireland and was welcomed at the Scottish court in November the same year. He continued to be promoted by the Scots in 1496 and there were border raids against the English. Until the Cornish rebellion distracted him in June 1497, Henry was preparing for a campaign against the Scots. Ultimately neither country could afford to get drawn into war and it was Spanish agents at the Scottish court who were instrumental in ending the deadlock. Ferdinand needed English support in the Holy League against France (mentioned below) and he was still committed to pursuing the Anglo-Spanish marriage. Eventually Warbeck left Scotland in June 1497 and the Truce of Ayton was signed, ending the state of war between the two countries. Relations were subsequently strengthened by the 1502 Treaty of Ayton and marriage alliance, resulting in the wedding of Margaret and James IV in 1503. Henry's security was certainly strengthened by peace on his northern border, closing Scotland to Yorkist claimants.

Henry's influence on the continent was very much derived from the fear created by French ambitions. Charles VIII's invasion of Italy and his dramatic early victories had caused real alarm by 1495 and the defensive League of Venice was established involving Ferdinand, Maximilian, Pope Alexander VI, Milan and Venice. Although Henry was not a party to this agreement, Ferdinand in particular saw Henry as a useful ally against the French and wanted to involve England in the

Holy League. To win English support, Burgundy and the Holy Roman Empire were persuaded to drop their backing of Yorkist exiles formally and trade was restored between England and Burgundy in an agreement known as *Intercursus Magnus*. This gave more scope to English merchants who could sell their goods freely anywhere in the territories of the Duke of Burgundy, with the exception of Flanders, without paying customs duties. By July 1496 Spanish persistence had paid off and Henry became an associate of the Holy League (the re-formed League of Venice), but he was able to maintain some independence and English relations with France were not jeopardised. When Louis XII acceded to the French throne in April 1498 and sought to renew the Italian campaign, Henry found himself being favoured by all the main powers. An agreement was reached between Henry and Louis in August that year, renewing and confirming the terms of the Treaty of Etaples.

Anglo-Spanish relations peaked in 1500 when a second marriage of Catherine and Arthur finally went ahead, by proxy, as Arthur reached the age of consent (14). Such ceremonies seem bizarre today, but they were an important part of the diplomatic process and were solemn and binding. The proxy who stood in for the absent bride was Doctor De Puebla, taking the right hand of the Prince of Wales in the ceremony. Haggling over the terms of Catherine's dowry continued to the last minute but Catherine finally arrived in England in late 1501 followed by her marriage in person. Henry appeared to have triumphed in securing the future of his dynasty, but all was seemingly shattered just five months later, when Arthur died, leaving a 16-year-old widow.

1502–07

Mortality and concerns about the succession shaped foreign policy in the final years of the reign. The pattern of diplomacy changed rapidly. Henry VII was left reacting to a bewildering number of developments which were beyond his control. Henry's diplomacy had a tired feel to it and he was often vulnerable and isolated. After the death of Isabella of Castile it became apparent that the Anglo-Spanish relationship was not that deep-rooted. Despite constant effort in these years Henry had limited concrete success. However, to his credit the ancient enmity and distrust between England and France and England and Scotland remained suppressed. Again, this reflects his realism: he did not want to jeopardise sound relations with France. In his maturity, the last thing he wanted was a debilitating, costly conflict with his powerful, close neighbour.

The table on pages 107–9 outlines the main developments in foreign relations from 1502. On the surface it appears that the widower King Henry was 'shopping around' to conclude a marriage treaty for himself, as well as for his son Henry, Prince of Wales and his second daughter, Mary. Possible brides for Henry VII included Joanna of Naples, Margaret of Savoy and Joanna of Castile. It is now thought unlikely that Henry ever seriously considered marrying the widowed Princess of Wales, Catherine of Aragon. However, rumours at the time were significant enough to reach an outraged Isabella. The source below shows how a monarch corresponded with a diplomat passing on her instructions to the English court.

◢ Source

The doctor (de Puebla) has ... written to us concerning the marriage of the King of England with the Princess of Wales, our daughter, saying that it is spoken of in England. But as this would be a very evil thing, one never before seen and the mere mention of which offends the ears – we would not for anything in the world that it should take place. Therefore, if anything be said to you about it, speak of it as a thing not to be endured. You must likewise say very decidedly that on no account would we allow it ...

The Calendar of State Papers, Spanish Vol. 1,
Henry VII 1485–1509 *(ed. G. A. Bergenroth), 1862*

The main point to remember is that all these largely fruitless marriage negotiations were bound up with Henry's overall desire for dynastic security and strategic advantage. For example, the proposed marriage of Henry to Joanna of Castile was intended to bring about an alliance of Burgundy, Spain and England against France.

	England	Burgundy	France	Spain
1502	Sept: Treaty with Spain – outlining terms for marriage.			Monarchs agree to open talks for Catherine's betrothal to Henry Prince of Wales.
1503	Feb: Death of Elizabeth of York – increased dynastic worries. Henry begins to seek marriage alliance for himself.		Relations between France and Spain beginning to deteriorate again.	Treaty of betrothal between Catherine and Henry signed in June. Ferdinand still in need of the English alliance.
1504	Henry was now faced with the prospect of trying to maintain the support of Philip and Ferdinand.	Philip wanted to add King of Castile to his titles. Burgundy and Aragon now rivals.	Treaty of Blois – between France and Spain (Ferdinand).	Oct: death of Isabella. Daughter Joanna inherited Castile, encouraged by her husband Philip, Duke of Burgundy. Ferdinand excluded from Castile.
1505	Henry pursued better relations with Burgundy where Edmund de la Pole, Earl of Suffolk, was. Improved trading links with Antwerp also advantageous.	Philip's claim to occupy the Castilian throne was backed by Henry		Ferdinand antagonised by closer Anglo-Burgundian relations. Marriage of Henry and Catherine looked unlikely.

	England	Burgundy	France	Spain
1506	Feb: Henry pressured Philip into signing the Treaty of Windsor – an alliance which committed Henry to the Habsburg cause. Suffolk to be surrendered to England. Marriage of Henry to Margaret of Savoy, Philip's sister, to be pursued. Henry's diplomatic strategy was thrown into confusion by death of Philip.	Diverted accidentally by a storm, Philip and Joanna entertained at the English court, where Henry took the opportunity to negotiate an alliance. Sept: Philip died. His six-year-old son Charles inherited the Burgundian title. Margaret of Savoy became regent in the Netherlands, but Maximilian, Holy Roman Emperor, had controlling influence.	France strengthened by the split between Ferdinand and Philip.	Ferdinand married Germaine de Foix, niece of Louis XII. Philip's widow, Joanna, was presumed insane. Ferdinand was now Regent of Castile, strengthening his position.
1507	Henry proposed a marriage between himself and widowed Joanna, ignoring rumours of her insanity. Idea	Dec: Treaty for the marriage of Mary Tudor and Archduke Charles agreed.		Ferdinand was still stalling on the details of Catherine's marriage to Henry. Relations between Ferdinand and Henry poor.

	England	Burgundy	France	Spain
	of marriage between his second daughter, Mary, and Charles also put forward.			
1508	Henry tried to form a triple alliance with France and the Habsburgs, isolating Ferdinand. This failed when England was left out of the League of Cambrai. Ultimately, Henry remained on terms with the main powers of Europe, but his influence was limited as his health deteriorated.	Dec: Maximilian and Archduke Charles were also signatories of the League of Cambrai, along with the Pope.	Louis XII involved in forming the League of Cambrai against Venice. He used bribes to get Ferdinand to join as he was worried about jeopardising his deal with the Spanish King over Italy.	Dec: the League of Cambrai was signed. Ferdinand was encouraged to join. Links with England not broken entirely, enabling marriage of Henry, Prince of Wales, and Catherine to eventually go ahead – after Henry's death.

TASKS

1 A tour around Europe in 1485

Investigate this by researching the situation in one or more of the territories listed below. Use the questions which then follow as a checklist to guide your research. You should be prepared to present your findings to the rest of your group, so that you can all put together an overall picture. Your group may decide to turn this exercise into a role play in which each of you is a diplomat reporting back to Henry VII (your teacher). In this case, you will need to concentrate particularly on questions a–f below. Take care not to upset the King!

◢ France
◢ Brittany
◢ Burgundy
◢ Spain
◢ Portugal
◢ Holy Roman Empire
◢ Scotland

You should decide what you want to know before you start. For this exercise you need to find out:

a Where the country is. Study the map of Western Europe in about 1485 on page 96.
b The name of the ruling family and ruler in 1485.
c The type of government the country has and how strong the central ruling authorities are.
d Does the ruler have claims to other territories or ambitions to gain more land?
e The main financial and commercial strengths and weaknesses of the state.
f Relationships with other states. Have relations between this country and England traditionally been good? Is an alliance with England likely to be useful for this country in 1485?

Before you start your investigation, this seems like a good time to remind you of some useful points for carrying out personal research in history:

◢ ALWAYS write the title, author and library catalogue number of any book you use – you might want to find it again.

◢ DO NOT repeat basic information you have from other books or class notes, but cross-reference these to your new reading.

◢ ALWAYS look up (or ask about) any word you meet that you do not know. How else does your vocabulary grow?

◢ As in this piece of research on Europe, read more general books first to give you an overview. For an essay you may want to tackle more specialised texts.

◢ Get used to using the table of contents and index in a text to focus your reading to what is relevant for your research.

◢ If you want to use the actual words of the book you are using, say so, like a quotation in a literature essay.

2 Essay planning

Essays often pick selected words and phrases and then ask you to show to what extent you agree that this is a valid judgement of some aspect of a monarch's reign. In this example you are asked to consider the following statement:

'A cautious and defensive response to changing circumstances.'
Discuss this view of Henry VII's foreign policy. (University of Cambridge Local Examinations Syndicate, June 1993)

By studying Henry's relations with other countries you will be able to gather evidence which supports or challenges the accuracy of such a statement. It is often an idea to tabulate your ideas which enables you to provide a balance of interpretations and opinions in your answer. It will also help you to avoid the temptation to write a chronological narrative of Henry's foreign policy.

As practice, try completing the table below. You may find you can link the same action or event with more than one of the descriptions. However, it is worthwhile trying to cover all the main foreign policy developments: after all, the examiner will expect you to reveal comprehensive knowledge of the period.

Words used to describe Henry's foreign policy	Evidence which can be used in support of this claim	Evidence which can be used to refute this claim
cautious and wary		
defensive		
pragmatic		
realistic		
decisive		
forward-thinking strategist		
unambitious	Henry had no territorial ambitions and he was preoccupied with a need for military glory, although he never formally gave up his claim to the French throne.	

3 Now consider this second essay title:

'In foreign affairs, Henry VII sought both security for his dynasty and trade advantages for England, but the former was always more important.' Discuss this verdict. (University of Cambridge Local Examinations Syndicate, June 1993)

Such an essay title is encouraging you to reveal your knowledge and understanding of Henry's foreign policy, whilst showing an awareness that domestic threats to the security of the dynasty and contacts with foreign powers were indistinguishable. You are being asked to analyse the motivation for Henry's actions. It also encourages you to identify links between other aspects of the reign. In this case you should examine how financial interests and the development of English trade conflicted with and were undermined by dynastic threats.

CHAPTER SIX

THE REIGN OF HENRY VII: WAS THIS THE NEW MONARCHY?

Objectives

⊿ To reach a conclusion about whether the reign of Henry VII was a turning point in English history

⊿ To examine whether the concept of 'new monarchy' has any value in defining the government of Henry VII.

Sometimes you might think recent historians have made studying a reign unnecessarily complicated. If you had studied history in the nineteenth century you would have had neat, coherent developments presented to you. Clear, convenient turning points were provided with straightforward causes. It is now impossible to neglect the varying interpretations of so-called revisionist historians, writing since the 1970s, who have challenged traditional assumptions. The reign of Henry VII might appear relatively uncontroversial in comparison with other Tudor monarchs, but it has not escaped debate. At issue is whether the system of government developed in a distinctive way during the reign, bringing in a new era of English kingship. Was Henry essentially following the pattern of medieval kingship, or was his Tudor monarchy the beginning of something new? Most historians have focused particularly on Henry's firm treatment of the nobility, his financial management and restoration of law and order to suggest this was the start of the modern state. Henry VII's new beginning thus meant stronger and more efficient rule.

Recent historians have questioned this claim of effective governance. They state that Henry's lack of instinctive trust in his natural partners, the nobility, undermined local order. This also meant that troubling plots and rebellions stretched unnecessarily over most of the reign. This approach has been put forward by Caroline Carpenter in *The Wars of the Roses: Politics and the Constitution in England 1437–1509* (CUP, 1997). She asserts that misleading conclusions about the reasons for Henry's achievement have in the past been reached by Tudor historians. They have approached the reign as the beginning of something new, rather than from the late medieval perspective it requires. Thus the reign of Henry VII has often appeared to be something different to the preceeding Yorkist governments, because of the differing approaches that Tudor and medieval historians have to research.

The focus of Carpenter's study is Henry VII's interactions with the nobility and gentry. An overview of the way the debate on Henry VII is now developing is also provided. Henry's differing approach towards the traditional powers of the nobility is not disputed, considering his exile, which meant unfamiliarity with the bulk of the existing nobility and the workings of local political society. However, new interpretations assert that Henry's preference for rewarding only a few close followers did not strengthen the Crown. As you have seen earlier, the Stanleys were among the favoured few who were hugely rewarded after Bosworth. Lord Stanley became the Earl of Derby and was granted extensive powers and lands in the north east. Jasper Tudor, given the Dukedom of Bedford, was granted significant influence and responsibilities for South Wales and the Marches. A few other Lancastrians had their earldoms restored, but most existing nobles were not favoured or trusted, as Henry's extensive use of bonds reveals. The implication of this, according to Carpenter, is that too much freedom was given to those he did trust and they were protected from their misuse of power. This in turn created contempt for the system of justice and in some areas evidence of feuding amongst favoured men is revealed.

Henry's dependence on trusted advisers of gentry origin, who owed their loyalty to him alone, is also re-examined. These men were given responsibility for asserting the King's will throughout the country. For councillors like Reginald Bray, this provided the opportunity to acquire lands which enhanced their authority and undermined existing local power structures, and hence the maintenance of order. Other trusted councillors included leading churchmen like John Morton and Richard Fox (Bishop of Durham). Despite the wide ranging influence of these advisers, recent interpretations have tended to support the view presented in this book that Henry's reign is chiefly characterised by his unwavering personal involvement in ruling the country.

The 'new monarchy' concept was first used by the nineteenth-century historian, J. R. Green, as part of the Victorian approach of dividing history into neat periods and imposing order on the past. He actually argued that the process of change began in the reign of the Yorkist king, Edward IV, and was largely completed with the political and religious upheavals of the Reformation Parliament (1529–36). During this period the power of kings began to grow at the expense of liberties established by parliament since the reign of Edward I; namely no arbitrary taxation, legislation or imprisonment without parliamentary consent. As a consequence the feudal constraints on kings grew weaker.

More recent historians have undermined the 'new monarchy' theory in various ways. In the 1950s Geoffrey Elton argued that the development of the institutions of governance came later, in the 1530s, with the so-called 'Tudor Revolution in Government', instituted by Thomas Cromwell. This thesis has itself been repudiated by those who have stressed continuity with medieval institutions and the limitations of government authority which lasted throughout the sixteenth century. J. R. Lander considers that 'it was the seventeenth, not the fifteenth century that, in England, saw the transition from the medieval to the modern state' (*Conflict and Stability in Fifteenth-Century England*, Hutchinson, 1977). Recent revisionists have stressed evolution rather than revolution. S. J. Gunn, for example, argues that Henry VII was simply using existing royal powers more efficiently, in response to the demand for more stable government and maintenance of law and order.

Historians studying European history of the comparative period also use the term 'new monarchy' in a general way to describe changes in government and the growth in power of centralised institutions. Across Europe monarchs were increasing their control and using pomp and display to mark themselves out from their subjects. In Spain and France this was the period when parliaments lost all chance of taking control. Monarchs in these countries were exploiting the breakdown of feudal relationships and a more sophisticated economy, based on credit, to fund patronage and hence win support from a wider base of people throughout their territories. However, even historians of European history have added qualifications to their use of the 'new monarchy', arguing that although European monarchies did become more powerful and increase their military resources, they did not become centralised modern states in the sixteenth century.

Other cultural and intellectual changes were also transforming European society from 'medieval' to 'modern'. Henry VII lived at the time of the Renaissance, which brought a questioning attitude to all aspects of life among the educated classes. Humanists discussed and debated issues such as the purpose of life on earth, and the place of humankind in the divine plan. In this sense Henry VII could be described as differing from some of the thinking and style of his predecessors, but it would be wrong to describe him as a 'Renaissance king'. However, he was not isolated from cultural developments as they spread north. As you have read in Chapter 4, Henry's increasing wealth meant that he could indulge his taste for architecture and other intellectual interests. Henry's court enjoyed Italian classical influences in art, music, literature and science: at the same time, vernacular English culture also flourished. There was certainly a new feel to the court of Henry VII, with considerable investment in pageantry and spectacle to reflect the glory and power of the King. He was prepared to be open-minded and embrace new ideas if it suited him personally. This had little bearing on his methods of government, but it does counter the traditional view of Henry as a serious-minded and grasping miser. Henry himself was only too willing to accept 'gifts of hawks and greyhounds. Henry was so fond of hunting that he kept at least five falconers on his chamber staff and as late as September 1507 (when he was 50) went hawking or hunting every day.' (Ian Dawson in *History Review*, September 1995).

In deciding whether Henry VII was in any way part of a trend of innovation you will need to think about the following changes in ways of governing, which have been put forward as evidence of a 'new monarchy':

◢ Centralisation of power: the traditional independence of the regions was reduced.
◢ Law and order was increasingly brought under the control of central institutions.
◢ The King increased his power, becoming ***autocratic*** and undermining the power of the nobles, particularly in the regions, replacing them with the support of the rising 'middle class'.
◢ Systems of government, such as management of Crown finances, were developed and became more efficiently managed.

⬧ Increased use of parliament, both as a source of revenue and as a counter-weight to the power of the nobility.

KEY TERM

Autocratic rulers possess authority unrestricted by any institution or group.

You will come to realise in your historical studies that firm conclusions on the methods and style of any reign cannot be neatly categorised. Change in governing institutions happened gradually, often unpredictably and was at no point irreversible, even though it might appear to have been, using the benefits of hindsight.

Henry VII's reign appears neat and efficient, so it is easy to imagine that he planned everything carefully and was unsurprised by his own success. You know, however, how anxious he became at the time of the Warbeck rebellion; how grasping and relentless his policies became after the death of his wife; and the extent to which foreign threats continued to preoccupy him. How much of his success was due to his careful planning and good judgement, and how much to luck? Were the ordinary people so tired of unrest, after the years of civil war, that they were prepared to accept firm government, even if it meant a reduction in freedom? Or did they regard a strong king as the desired norm? Sir John Fortescue, writing in the 1470s, commented that a weak King like Henry VI was not how government should be, and that a strong monarch would simply restore normality.

Whether you are studying Henry VII as the culmination of your studies of fifteenth-century Lancastrian and Yorkist monarchies, or at the beginning of your studies of Tudor monarchy, you will need to reach your own conclusions as to the significance of the reign of Henry VII within the wider context of change and continuity.

Examining the views of historians

1 Read through the groups of extracts below. Most of these are taken from texts that were written for academics, so although you are likely to find copies of some of them in your school/college library, the language is occasionally challenging. It is worth persevering with them: look up any words you do not know and think about the context in which they are used.

2 From each extract, identify the main points. Set out your summary of the views of each in a table like the one below, using the headings given.

	Evidence for or against the 'new monarchy'	View of significance of the reign
(A) G. R. Elton, 1955		
(B) R. L. Storey, 1968		
(C) S. B. Chrimes, 1972		
(D) A. Goodman, 1988		
(E) John Guy, 1988		
(F) S. J. Gunn, 1995		
(G) R. Lockyer and A. Thrush, 1997		

3 On what points do the extracts agree or disagree?

4 Now go back and review your own ideas on whether Henry was medieval, or beginning a new era of modern kingship, from your

TASKS

studies of Henry's methods of government and finance covered in Chapters 3 and 4.

Extracts from historians

◢ Extract A

It would, however, be quite wrong to suppose, on the one hand, that Henry VII made himself a deliberately 'middle-class' king, or – on the other hand – that he invariably deferred to the interests of gentry and merchants. The most obvious way in which Henry's kingship differed from that of his predecessors was in the greater stress he laid upon it. Even this far from impressive-looking man fostered the visible dignity of the office and took good care that the greatest of his subjects should appear small by his side ...

It is also commonly asserted that Henry VII innovated when he surrounded himself with a council of men from the 'middle class'. As a matter of fact, Henry's council of men included noblemen – Lancastrians like the Earls of Oxford and Ormond, and reprieved Yorkists like the Earl of Surrey. It included new creations like Giles Lord Daubeney who came from the upper ranks of the gentry ... The Tudors were not against aristocracy as such; they were against obstreperous men, whether noble or gentle or common.

From G. R. Elton **England under the Tudors** (Methuen, 1955)

◢ Extract B

The reign of Henry VII must still be regarded as one of the great landmarks in England's political development. Historians asking themselves whether he was 'medieval' or a 'modern' type of king have found their answer by examining the organisation of his administration. This is the wrong yardstick. Henry was not the last king to be intimately concerned with the work of government; he may have applied himself more diligently to its details than his successors, but several of his predecessors equally lacked his powers of concentration to business. If previous kings had been less authoritarian and stringent, it was not because they were endowed with fewer prerogatives but rather because their administrative organisations were less efficient or they preferred, or were compelled, to rule with looser reins.

From R. L. Storey **The Reign of Henry VII** (Blandford Press, 1968)

Figure 9 An anonymous portrait of Henry VII with his two councillors, Richard Empson and Edmund Dudley

◢ Extract C

His was not an original mind; he was no great innovator. He was rather a highly skilful builder on existing foundations, an eclectic adopter and adapter. He could bring an essentially medieval spirit and practice of government to its highest point of effectiveness without in any important way changing its character. A lover of power he certainly was, but to wield power was his vocation and his destiny ... his services to the realm were immeasurable, far greater than he himself could have imagined or predicted. His régime produced a pacification, an orderliness, a cohesion, a viability in the forms and machinery of government, a sustained effectiveness without which stability and consolidation could not have been obtained, and provided an indispensable standpoint for subsequent growth and flowering.

From S. B. Chrimes **Henry VII** (1972)

◢ Extract D

The return to the Commons of large numbers of royal retainers was also helpful. Shire knights and burgesses apparently negotiated the grant of subsidies without much

demur; they showed no inclination to follow precedents of attempting to control the expenditure of subsidies, or of interfering in the personnel and policies of government. Out of parliament as well as in it the elites tended to give a more habitual and uncritical loyalty to the ruler. Magnate families ceased to provide an alternative focus for loyalties, partly as a result of accidents of inheritance, but also because the Tudors, though not 'anti-noble', were determined that magnate power should be used to sustain rather than undermine the authority of the law. There was, indeed, as a result of a variety of factors ..., a swing in the balance of power from magnates to crown. But this was not the result of an alliance between the Crown and a rising 'middle class'... The striking institutional and political achievements of the ... Tudors ... can be plausibly represented as revivals and renovations rather than the establishment of a new monarchy. Moreover, the idea of a new monarchy as propounded by Green ... was alien to contemporaries. Indeed, it is not surprising that kings and councillors failed to project themselves as innovators; the concept of novelty was in itself unattractive to subjects, especially in constitutional matters.

From Anthony Goodman **The New Monarchy England, 1471–1534**, Historical Association Studies (1988)

◢ Extract E

Henry also attempted to centralise English politics. The Tudor Court began to exercise magnetic influence, and if much territorial power still lay in the hands of regional magnates, faction was tamed by recognisance and the exaction of royal prerogative rights by the Council Learned. Lastly, Henry's diplomacy and security measures guaranteed his dynasty's survival. The turbulence of the fifteenth century was quelled.

From John Guy **Tudor England** (1988)

◢ Extract F

Financial strength, whether derived from an enlarged crown estate or from intensified direct taxation, was made possible by tighter supervision of local elites, but in turn it facilitated expenditure – on magnificence, war, patronage and the suppression of rebellion – to make such supervision more palatable or less resistible. The growth of the state in the minds of its subjects, albeit fragmentary, encouraged the loyalty that submitted to political control, cooperated in the king's judicial enterprise, and paid taxes.

Many of the institutions and devices central to these changes were in existence by 1400 or well before: ... JPs, a royal household acting as a royal affinity in the provinces, laws against retaining, directly assessed personal taxation and parliament itself, to name but a few. However, they had never been applied in the same way as they were by the kings from Edward IV on, nor in the same social and political context.

From S. J. Gunn *Early Tudor Government* (Macmillan, 1995)

◢ Extract G

It is true that Henry's government was efficient by the standards of its day, focused power upon the centre, and was autocratic to the extent that it stressed the royal authority and used a wide range of prerogative institutions and practices. It is also true that it worked through household institutions like the Chamber, rather than the Exchequer, and that its chief officials were drawn from the gentry rather than the nobility. In all these ways, then, Henry VII seems to conform to the pattern of a 'New Monarch'.

There is however, another side to the picture ... There are certainly centralising tendencies to be discerned in Henry VII's government, but what strikes a modern observer most about his administration is the way in which power was decentralised rather than concentrated ... The Council could advise, encourage, warn and threaten, but in the last resort Henry was dependent upon the cooperation of the propertied section of society.

Henry was never an absolute monarch. He was limited by custom and by law, and even had he wished to sweep away these barriers he could not have done so. He had no police force and no standing army ...

Henry's ... reliance on 'middle class' men is often put forward as the most novel feature of his reign, but ... these were not middle class: indeed the term itself was unknown. They belonged to the upper section of English society, the political nation, and were new only in the sense that their families had not previously been prominent in central administration ... He successfully founded a new dynasty but luck played a major part even in this: if Prince Henry had followed his brother Arthur to the grave, the peaceful accession of Henry's eldest daughter Margaret could not have been taken for granted, civil war might well have broken out again, and Henry VII would be remembered, if at all, simply as one more in the succession of late-medieval rulers who tried in vain to restore the strength of the monarchy and with it good order and government.

From Roger Lockyer and Andrew Thrush *Henry VII* (1997) (third edition)

FURTHER READING

M. Alexander *The First of the Tudors* (Rowman and Littlefield USA, 1980) – full of interesting details, and useful because it give precise dates, enabling the reader to see the links between different aspects.

Ian Arthurson *Documents of the Reign of Henry VII* (University of Cambridge Local Examinations Syndicate, 1984) – a wide and interesting range of sources, many of them complete rather than pre-digested and cut about!

Christine Carpenter *The Wars of the Roses: Politics and the Constitution in England 1437–1509* (CUP, 1997) – the views of a late medieval historian, she questions the long-held assumptions of Tudor historians and her conclusions are those of an 'unrepentant critic of the King'.

S. B Chrimes *Henry VII* (Methuen, 1972) – still the most thorough, academic study of Henry VII. Some of the 'technical' terms of the period are very closely defined.

Anthony Goodman *The New Monarchy* (Blackwell/Historical Association, 1988) – useful summary of historical discussions this century on the subject of how 'new' the system adopted by Henry VII was. Quite difficult in terms of vocabulary and concepts, but worth the effort!

R. A. Griffiths and R. S. Thomas *The Making of the Tudor Dynasty* (Alan Sutton, 1985) – a good read if you want to know more about the family background of the Tudors.

John Guy *Tudor England* (Oxford UP, 1988) – this is the definitive study, which embraces modern thinking on monarchy and government in Tudor times. Each chapter can be read on its own.

J. R. Lander *Government and Community: England 1450–1509* (Edward Arnold, 1980) – a thorough and detailed account of the reign, putting Henry firmly in the context of continuity with the Yorkists, and with interesting social and economic insights.

Roger Lockyer and Andrew Thrush *Henry VII* (Longman Seminar Studies, 1997) – interesting and readable account, with a useful conclusion on the significance of the reign. Also a range of primary sources. Recently revised to take into account new views.

Caroline Rogers *Henry VII* (Hodder and Stoughton, 1991) – a clearly set out discussion of the reign, with plenty of detail on topics like commerce and trade.

Polydore Vergil *The Anglica Historia 1485–1537* ed. D. Hay (London RHS Camden Series LXXIV, 1950) – interesting as one of the few primary sources which focus specifically on the reign of Henry VII; also full of readable character sketches and opinions.

Fiction and novels: for background

Josephine Tey *Daughter of Time* (Paladin paperback) – classic defence of Richard III in the form of a whoddunnit .

Anya Seton *Katherine* – life of the third wife of John of Gaunt, founder of the Beaufort dynasty.

William Shakespeare *Richard III* – early pro-Tudor propaganda piece, which turns the last of the Yorkist Kings into a bloodthirsty and irrational tyrant.

INDEX

KEY TERMS

MAIN INDEX

Longman History in Depth

Series editor: Christopher Culpin

Titles in the series

Hitler and Nazism (0 582 29736 2)

Causes of the Second World War (0 582 29650 1)

Stalin and the Soviet Union (0 582 29733 8)

Origins of the First World War (0 582 29522 X)

The Russian Revolution (0 582 29731 1)

Parnell and the Irish Question (0 582 29628 5)

Gladstone (0 582 29521 1)

Chartism (0 582 29735 4)

Oliver Cromwell (0 582 29734 6)

Charles I (0 582 29732 X)

Henry VII (0 582 29691 9)

Addison Wesley Longman Limited,
Edinburgh Gate, Harlow,
Essex,CM20 2JE, England
and Associated Companies throughout the world.

The right of Jocelyn Hunt and Carolyn Towle to be identified as the authors of this Work has been asserted by them in accordance with the Copyright, Designs and Patents Act of 1988.

First published 1998
© Addison Wesley Longman Limited 1998

Set in 9.5/13pt Stone Serif
Produced by Addison Wesley Longman Singapore Publisher Pte Ltd
Printed in Singapore

ISBN 0 582 29691 9

Acknowledgements

We are grateful to the following for permission to reproduce photographs:

Courtesy of the Dean and Chapter of Westminster, page 20 bottom; Mary Evans Picture Library, pages 45 left and right, 120; by courtesy of the National Portrait Gallery, London, page 20 top and centre; RCHME, © Crown Copyright, page 70; Topham Picturepoint, pages 34, 89.

Cover painting: Henry VII by Michael Sittow. National Portrait Gallery, London.

The publisher's policy is to use paper manufactured from sustainable forests.